EXPLORE DEATH VALLEY II
(Northern & Eastern)

Secret Places In The Mojave Desert: Volume VI

By Jim Mattern (aka. Death Valley Jim)
Photographs by the author (except where noted)
Historic Photos are public domain.
Cover photo: Strozzi Ranch
Back cover: Greenwater Canyon Pictographs

Copyright © 2015 Death Valley Jim

All rights reserved. No part of this publication may be reproduced, stored in a retrieval system, or transmitted, by any means, electronic, mechanical, photocopying, recording or otherwise – except as permitted under Section 107 or 108 of the United States Copyright Act – without the prior written permission of Death Valley Jim.

Dedication
Kenneth Johnson (1946-2015)

Ken is a person that I feel blessed to have had come into my life. The man was full of passion and love for the desert. He dedicated his time and resources to researching and protecting archeological and natural treasures in the southwest. Ken lost his life at the end of June, while doing what he loved. He is missed by myself, and the community that he served.

SPECIAL THANKS TO THE FOLLOWING:

Meghan Mattern, Sandy (mom) & Mike Scafedi, Mike Behrman, Ryan Halub, Seth Shteir and the NPCA, Tom & the Big O Tire crew in Yucca Valley, Amina Anderson (Beatty Museum), John Grasson (Dezert Magazine), Dr. Alan Garfinkel Gold, Ted Faye, Ranger "X", Nicholas Clapp, David Smith & George Land at Joshua Tree National Park, Buster Baker, Alisa Lynch & Rose Masters at Manzanar National Historic Site, The Band Perry, Jeffrey Spivey, Rajan Parrikar, Red Rock Books (Ridgecrest, CA), Desert Map & Aerial Photo (Palm Desert, CA), RR Broadcasting, KPTR, Andy @ SCORE, Coachellavalley.com, Bakersfield Magazine.

I'd also like to thank everyone that purchased this book, or other volumes. Those that read my website, follow me on Facebook, and listen to or have appeared on my radio program.

WARNING!

ABANDONED AND INACTIVE MINES
ARE DEATH TRAPS!
DON'T GET TRAPPED!

STAY OUT!

STAY ALIVE!

DANGERS AWAIT INSIDE:
- HIDDEN DEEP SHAFTS
- CAVE-INS OF LOOSE ROCK OR DECAYED TIMBERS
- UNSAFE OR BROKEN LADDERS
- BAD AIR AND POISONOUS GASES
- DISCARDED EXPLOSIVES
- POISONOUS SNAKES
- FLOODED TUNNELS

NOTE: This book is best used with mapping software, and a hand held GPS unit.

Mapping software could be anything from Google Earth, to software that comes with a handheld GPS when purchased (for instance Basecamp, which comes with all Garmins).

I use Google Earth when mapping and researching areas. Google Earth is available for free from: earth.google.com

I provide coordinates for every location in this book. The coordinates can be punched into a GPS device, or mapping software to allow you to find the location, and create routes to it.

Topographical maps have also been included. Please be aware that some of the maps may show roads that are no longer open.

The coordinate system used in this book is geographic coordinates (latitude/longitude) on the World Geodetic System of 1984 (WGS84) datum.

TABLE OF CONTENTS

A Word from the Author	1
Desert Travel Essentials	2
Etiquette for visiting "Rock Art"	3
Leave No Trace	4
NEVADA TRIANGLE	**8**
Bonnie Clair & Thorp	9
Bullfrog	13
Currie Well	16
Goldbar	19
Happy Hooligan Mine & Cave Rock Spring	20
Klair Spring Petroglyphs (California)	28
Leadfield (California)	30
Phinney Mine	36
Sarcobatus Spring Shelter	39
Strozzi Ranch	42
NORTHERN DEATH VALLEY	**50**
Crater Mine	51
Eureka Valley Overlook	53
Marble Bath	55
Mesquite Springs Petroglyphs	57
EASTERN PANAMINTS	**60**
Emigrant Canyon Petroglyphs	61
Grave of Frank Shorty Harris & James Dayton	65
Hungry Bill's Ranch & Johnson Canyon	69
Queen of Sheba Mine	74
Tucki Mine	79
GREENWATER	**84**
Funeral Petroglyphs	85
Greenwater Canyon Petroglyphs	89
Greenwater Canyon Pictographs	93

FUNERAL MOUNTAINS	100
Chloride City & Chloride Cliff	101
Echo Canyon Petroglyphs	107
Eye of the Needle	110
Inyo Mine	112
Schwab	117
SOUTHEAST OF DEATH VALLEY	122
Death Valley Junction	123
Dublin Gulch Caves	127
Noonday Mines & Camp	130
Restings Springs Pass Welded Tuff	134
Tecopa (Old) Aka: Brownsville	136
HISTORIC PHOTO ARCHIVE	140

A word from the author:

Death Valley National Park is a very special place to me. It was the first place that I fell in love with in the desert southwest. The vastness of the valley (or basin), the monsterous mountains that stand tall, and full of color - with over 5,000 acres (mostly of wilderness), there is an adventure to be had at every turn.

The book that you are about to read, has taken years to put together - it contains many sensitive, and or "secret" places, along with some of the more known, but "low-key" locations.

This is by no means an all-inclusive guide book. One could spend a lifetime exploring Death Valley National Park, and never see everything. What this is, is a damn good start - and should keep the casual visitor busy for many trips, and even the more "hardcore" visitor, busy for an extended period of time.

It is also worth mentioning that not all of the sites in the book are within the boundaries of the National Park, some sit on nearby BLM land. I made the decision to include these nearby sites because of their importance or uniqueness to the area.

Please remember to treat these places with respect. They are owned by all of the people of the United States, and we all have a responsibility to protect them - and the right to visit them.

On an additional sidenote: My writing style varies sometimes from entry to entry. Sometimes I provide a narrative, other times purely facts. I've never claimed to be a good writer, but never the less I enjoy what I do, and I hope that you will as well.

Thanks for reading,
Death Valley Jim

DESERT TRAVEL ESSENTIALS

The following are all items that should be carried with you when traveling in the desert. The list may sound like a lot, but in a worst case scenario you will want to be prepared. If you are not prepared you are risking your life, as well anyones life that may be traveling with you. This is in no way a complete list, but a good starting point.

Water - You can never bring too much! Some people recommend a gallon of water per person per day. I personally recommend a 5 gallon jug for every two people in your party per day.

Food - Always carry extra food that can last you a day or two. I keep enough prepackaged beef jerky with me to last a few days, it is light weight and compact. Self-Heating MRE's are also a wonderful option to keep packed in your vehicle for an emergency meal.

Shovel - My shovel stays in my vehicle at all times, even when I'm just cruising around town. You never know when you might get stuck.

Gasoline - There are long stretches of backcountry roads, and many times a gas station can be over a hundred miles away. Having some extra gasoline with you as a precaution is a good thing.

Handheld GPS or Compass- A handheld outdoor GPS is the only GPS that you should trust in the desert. Make sure it is loaded with topographical maps of the area that you are traveling, and make sure you know how to read them. DO NOT RELY ON YOUR VEHICLES GPS DEVICE.

Spare Tire or Two - No explanation needed. Don't forget the jack!

Matches/Lighter - Something that will allow you to start a fire easily.

Signal flares or mirror - Anything that might get the attention of an airplane flying overhead, or another motorist that you may see at a distance.

Knife or Multitool - A knife can come in handy in many situations. From skinning an animal, to helping build a shelter, or even using it as a signaling device.

First Aid Kid - Injuries happen when we least expect it. Be prepared for them! It is also important in a desert situation that you add a snake bite kit to your first aid kit.

Blanket/Warm Clothing - In the spring, winter and fall months temperatures at night can get downright cold. Sometimes well below freezing! Don't let the warm daytime temperatures fool you, and always be prepared for colder weather.

ETIQUETTE FOR VISITING ROCK ART

Petroglyphs & Pictographs are fragile, non-renewable cultural resources that, once damaged, can never be replaced.

By remembering and following the rules listed here, you can help preserve these unique and fragile cultural resources that are part of our heritage.

Avoid Touching the Petroglyphs & Pictographs

Look and observe, BUT DO NOT TOUCH! Preserve petroglyphs & pictographs by not touching them in any way. Even a small amount of the oils from our hands can erode petroglyphs & pictographs and destroy the patina (color) of the carved, pecked or painted image.

When climbing among the rocks be careful, you can dislodge loose stones causing damage to the petroglyph & pictograph boulders. Falling rocks may scratch the carved and pecked images causing unintentional damage. Do not re-arrange the rocks or move things from where you find them. The petroglyphs & pictographs are important individually and in relation to each other. To even try and understand a petroglyph or pictograph it needs to be viewed in relation to its environment: including the adjacent image(s), the entire basalt escarpment, and the surrounding landscape. For someone to fully appreciate a site, the glyphs and their surroundings should be left undisturbed.

Do not introduce any foreign substance to enhance the carved, pecked or painted images for photographic or drawing purposes. Altering, defacing, or damaging the petroglyphs is against the law — even if the damage is unintentional.

Re-pecking or re-painting does not restore a petroglyph or pictograph, it destroys the original. DO NOT add your own marks to the images. The introduction of graffiti destroys the petroglyphs & pictographs and is disrespectful to contemporary Native Americans and their ancestors.

Don't remove the petroglyphs & pictographs! It is against the law to remove items from prehistoric or geologic sites. Such vandalism carries a fine and penalty.

LEAVE NO TRACE

Plan Ahead and Prepare

- Know the regulations and special concerns for the area you'll visit.
- Prepare for extreme weather, hazards, and emergencies.
- Schedule your trip to avoid times of high use.
- Visit in small groups when possible. Consider splitting larger groups into smaller groups.
- Repackage food to minimize waste.
- Use a map and compass to eliminate the use of marking paint, rock cairns or flagging.

Travel and Camp on Durable Surfaces

- Durable surfaces include established trails and campsites, rock, gravel, dry grasses or snow.
- Protect riparian areas by camping at least 200 feet from lakes and streams.
- Good campsites are found, not made. Altering a site is not necessary.

In popular areas:

- Concentrate use on existing trails and campsites.
- Walk single file in the middle of the trail, even when wet or muddy.
- Keep campsites small. Focus activity in areas where vegetation is absent.

In pristine areas:

- Disperse use to prevent the creation of campsites and trails.
- Avoid places where impacts are just beginning.

Dispose of Waste Properly

- Pack it in, pack it out. Inspect your campsite and rest areas for trash or spilled foods. Pack out all trash, leftover food, and litter.
- Deposit solid human waste in catholes dug 6 to 8 inches deep at least 200 feet from water, camp, and trails. Cover and disguise the cathole when finished.
- Pack out toilet paper and hygiene products.
- To wash yourself or your dishes, carry water 200 feet away from streams or lakes and use small amounts of biodegradable soap. Scatter strained dishwater.

Leave What You Find

- Preserve the past: examine, but do not touch, cultural or historic structures and artifacts.
- Leave rocks, plants and other natural objects as you find them.
- Avoid introducing or transporting non-native species.
- Do not build structures, furniture, or dig trenches.

Minimize Campfire Impacts

- Campfires can cause lasting impacts to the backcountry. Use a light weight stove for cooking and enjoy a candle lantern for light.
- Where fires are permitted, use established fire rings, fire pans, or mound fires.
- Keep fires small. Only use sticks from the ground that can be broken by hand.
- Burn all wood and coals to ash, put out campfires completely, then scatter cool ashes.

Respect Wildlife

- Observe wildlife from a distance. Do not follow or approach them.
- Never feed animals. Feeding wildlife damages their health, alters natural behaviors, and exposes them to predators and other dangers.
- Protect wildlife and your food by storing rations and trash securely.
- Control pets at all times, or leave them at home.
- Avoid wildlife during sensitive times: mating, nesting, raising young, or winter.

Be Considerate of Other Visitors

- Respect other visitors and protect the quality of their experience.
- Be courteous. Yield to other users on the trail.
- Step to the downhill side of the trail when encountering pack stock.
- Take breaks and camp away from trails and other visitors.
- Let nature's sounds prevail. Avoid loud voices and noises.

Center for Outdoor Ethics | LNT.org

There are two deserts: One is a grim, desolate wasteland. It is the home of venomous reptiles and stinging insects, of vicious thorn-covered plants and trees and unbearable heat. This is the desert seen by the stranger speeding along the highway, impatient to be out of the "damnable country." It is the desert visualized by those children of luxury to whom any environment is intolerable which does not provide all the comforts and luxuries of a pampering civilization. It is the concept fostered by fiction writers who dramatize the tragedies of the desert because there is a market for such manuscripts.

But the stranger and the uninitiated see only the mask. The other desert - the real desert - is not for the eyes of the superficial observer or the fearful soul of a cynic. It is a land which reveals its true character only to those who come with courage, tolerance and understanding. For these, the desert holds rare gifts: a health-giving sunshine; a sky that after the sun goes down is studded with diamonds; a breeze that bears no poison; a landscape of pastel colors such as no artist can reproduce; thorn-covered plants which during countless ages have clung tenaciously to life through heat, drought, wind and the depredations of thirsty animals, and each season send forth blossoms of exquisite coloring as symbols of courage that triumphed over appalling obstacles.

To those who come to the desert with tolerance it gives friendliness; to those who come with courage it gives new strength of character. Those seeking relaxation find in its far horizons and secluded canyons release from the world of man-made tensions. For those seeking beauty the desert offers nature's rarest artistry. This is the desert that has a deep and lasting fascination for men and women with a bit of poetry in their souls.

-Randall Henderson (Desert Magazine)

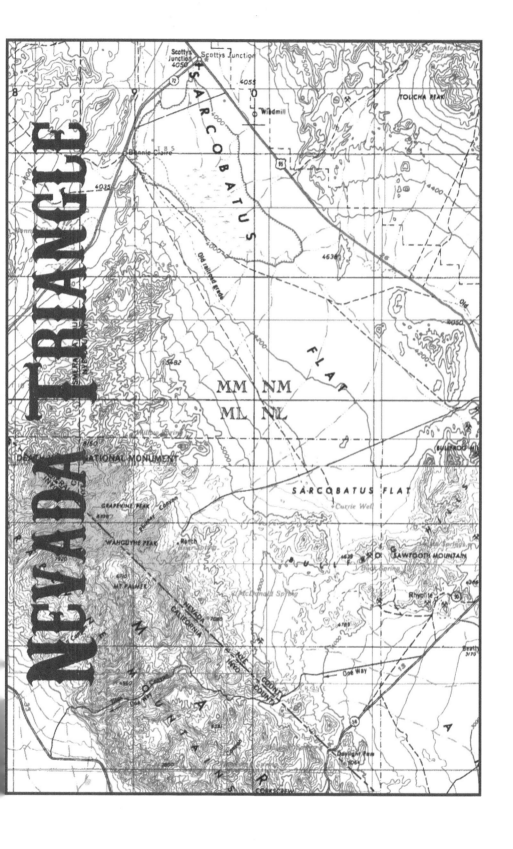

BONNIE CLAIR & THORP

GPS Coordinates: 37°13'35.73"N 117° 7'16.18"W

Mining began in the area around 1880 about four miles from what would become the town site of Thorp and later Bonnie Claire. The earliest name for the mining area was Thorp's Well, and is what the original town name is derived from. In the early 1900's the Bonnie Clare and Bullfrog Mining Company purchased the mill at Thorp's Well, and soon afterwards began construction of a new mill near the Thorp Stage Station. This new mill would be called the Bonnie Claire Mill.

The town of Thorp was established around 1904, with the first post office opening in 1905. The town would be renamed Bonnie Claire in 1906 after the arrival of the Bullfrog and Goldfield Railroad. In 1907 the Las Vegas and Tonopah Railroad would reach the town.

1907 saw the peak of the town's population at about one-hundred people. The town site now had a two-story hotel, a number of saloons and stores, and houses had begun to be built to replace the tent city. Despite the small boom that had taken place due to the trains reaching the town it wasn't long before the town began to diminish.

Bonnie Claire would see another busy period in the 1920's, when Chicago Millionaire Albert Johnson and Walter Scott (Death Valley Scotty) began construction on what would become known as Scotty's Castle.

Most of the supplies for the construction of the castle came through Bonnie Claire via the railroad, and was then trucked out twenty desolate miles to the construction site. When the Great Depression hit construction on the mansion would decrease, which would again cause an exodus.

Eventually the railroad tracks leading through Bonnie Claire were pulled up, and the train stopped rolling through this once bustling little town. In 1931 the town would lose their post office.

Today the town site consists of a couple of lonely buildings that have been littered with modern-day garbage, and modern era junk cars. A small mining shaft is located directly beside one of the buildings, it's unclear if this shaft was used in the early days of Bonnie Claire, or if it's from a more recent time.

Across the highway the Bonnie Claire mill still stands proudly against the mountain as well as a number of adobe structures. The old mill's smelting pots rest on the ground beside the mill giving testimony to the mill's once bustling history.

Tonopah and Tidewater No. 12 at Bonnie Claire Depot. Date unknown.

Above: Bonnie Claire Mill, 1908.
Below: The ruins of the Bonnie Claire Mill.

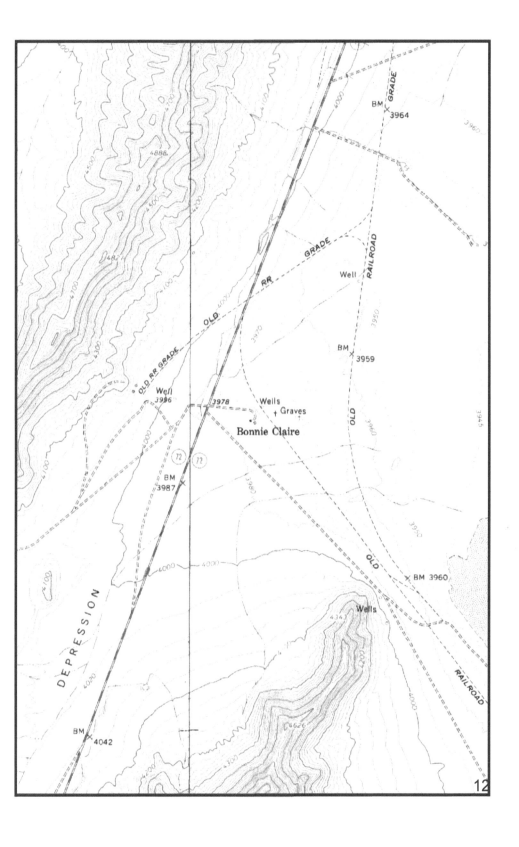

BULLFROG

GPS Coordinates: 36°53'23.96"N 116°50'4.46"W

Bullfrog came to be in March 1905 when the entire town of Amargosa City packed up and moved to the Bullfrog town site. A short time later Rhyolite was established within just a mile of Bullfrog. The competition between the two towns was fierce, both towns wanted the edge on the other. May of 1905 would end up the peak of Bullfrog as a town. Lots on main street sold for as much as $1,500. Bullfrog also boasted a three-story hotel, a county jail, a lodging house, a general store, a bank, and an ice house among others.

It has often been said that the town of Bullfrog was a violent town; the violence attributed to the town folks and businesses packing up and leaving for Rhyolite. By 1907 Bullfrog was practically deserted. The post office struggled but managed to stay open until May, 15th 1909.

Today not much remains of Bullfrog. Rhyolite is still over shadowing it some one-hundred years later. The walls of the ice house remain, and a good part of the county jail is still intact.

Ruins of the jail at Bullfrog.

Bullfrog, NV – Date unknown, people unknown.

Bullfrog, NV in November of 1906.

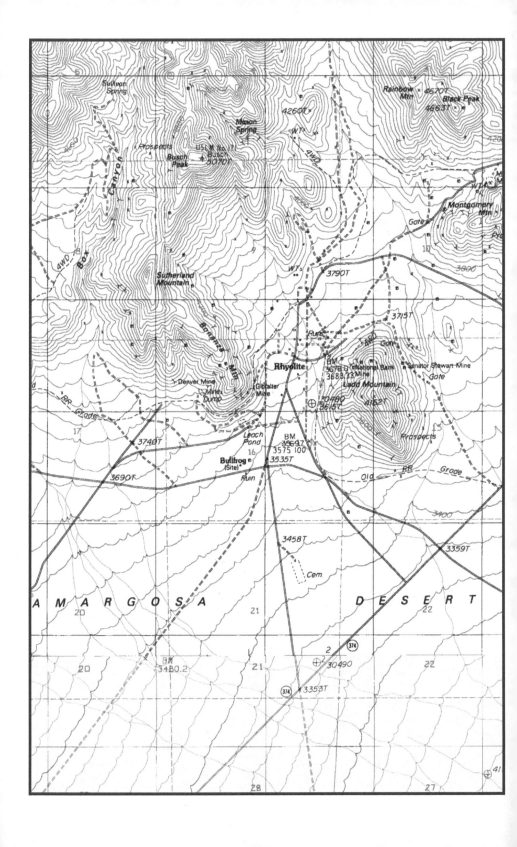

CURRIE WELL

GPS Coordinates: 36°58'9.60"N 116°55'36.21"W

Bouncing down the roads of Death Valley's Nevada Triangle there are a plethora of historic sites to discover, many of them are small ghost camps from the late 1800's on into the depression era. Most have been reduced to nothing more than can scatters, but that is alright, can scatters can tell a lot about a site, from its age to approximately how many people utilized an area, and for how long. Currie Well is one of these such sites.

Currie Well is located eleven miles north of Rhyolite, and was first used as a watering hole for miners and travelers along the route to or from Goldfield. Between 1907-1909 some crude business men attempted to profit off of the water at Currie Well, charging travelers for water, and selling meals and forage for their animals. Also in 1907 the Las Vegas & Tonopah Railroad built a work camp on the site during the construction of the railroad. Once construction was completed, the camp was torn down.

The water was obtained from three different wells in the vicinity, at the depths of 10, 12, and 14 feet. These wells provided 200 barrels of "excellent water" daily.

Ruins of a beehive furnace at Currie Well.

In 1909 a last-ditch effort was made by the owner of the water source to increase flow, and pipe water to local mines. This didn't last long as many of the mines in the region proved unsuccessful.

...and that is the short-lived story of Currie Well.

Currie Well today has been reduced to mostly scattered cans, and pipes. A historic junkyard at best. The most significant remaining traces of the past are two beehive style furnaces. They were most likely used by railroad construction workers as blacksmith forges, however some historians believe that they were used to smelt ore from area mines.

Located south east of Currie Well the old railroad bed of the Las Vegas & Tonopah Railroad can be found. Some reports indicate that it can be driven, however I question that due to area wilderness boundaries.

Extensive rusty relics at Currie Well.

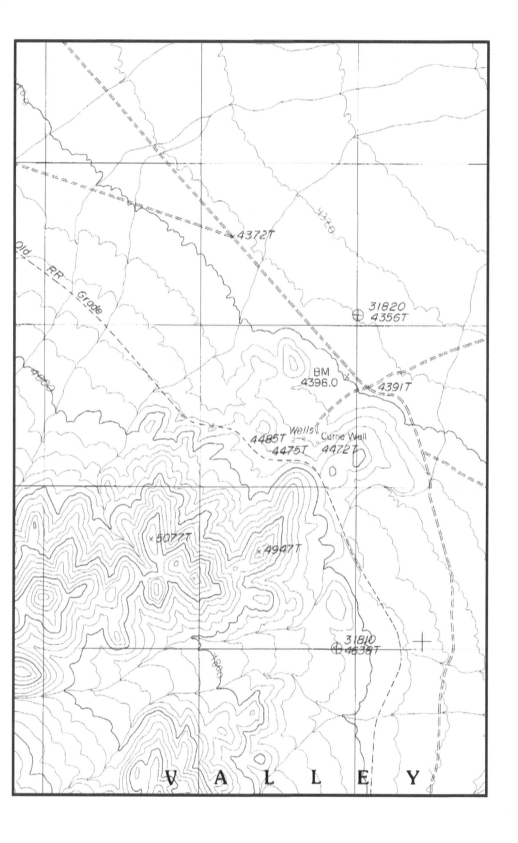

Gold Bar

GPS Coordinates: 36°56'20.06"N 116°53'13.17"W

Gold Bar, NV is located in the Bullfrog mining district near the ghost town of Rhyolite, NV. Today it sits within the boundaries of Death Valley National Park.

Gold Bar came to be around 1905, as another of many small mining camps located in the Bullfrog Mining District. The camp had an estimated population of around fifty people in its heyday. Despite never graduating from a camp to a town, a number of substantial structures had been built-in hopes of promoting growth.

The Homestake Mine & Mill were the mainstays of the camp. The ore that was mined, was said to be rich and worth as much as $150 per ton. In 1908 the recession was hitting Gold Bar hard and in May of that year the Homestake Mine & Mill closed for good. It would later be discovered that the mine was falsely promoted, and its ore was worthless.

Today the only remains of Gold Bar is the massive foundation of the Homestake Mill. Without the mill foundation you would never know that anything existed here.

Foundation ruins of the Homestake Mill.

Gold Bar circa 1905-1906.

The Gold Bar Mine and Mill in 1908.

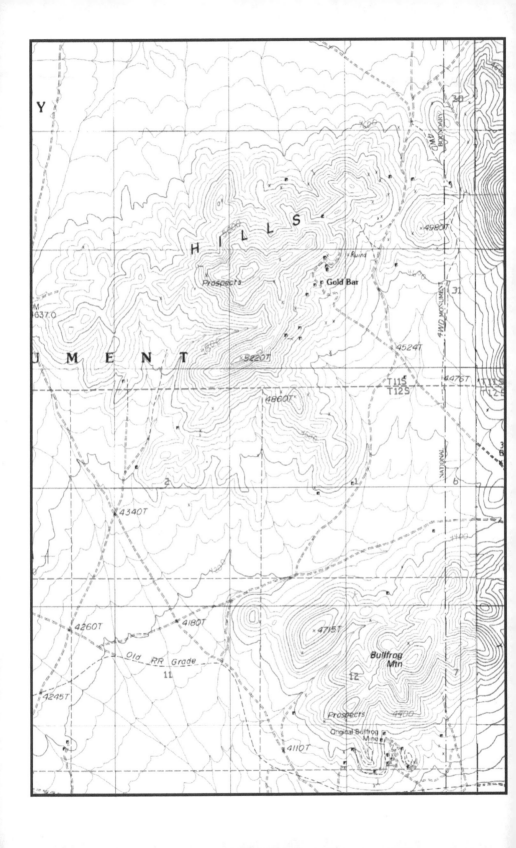

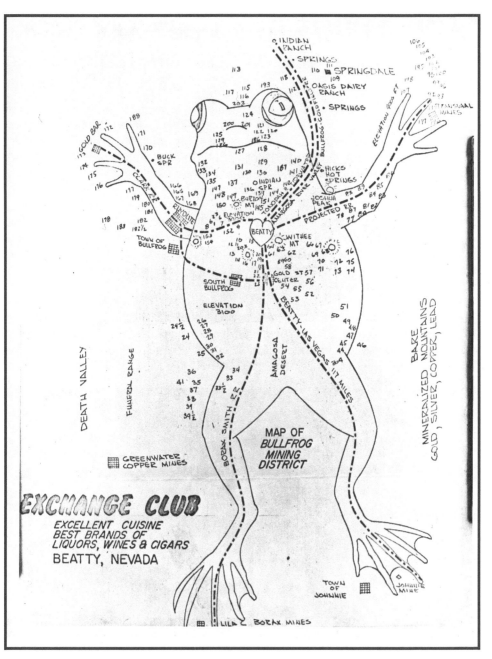

The famous map of Bullfrog Mining District, designed by T.G. Nicklin, editor Of the Bullfrog Miner, Beatty, Nevada, shortly after the founding of the town of Beatty. This particular copy was distributed by the Exchange Club, probably During the 1950s. The town of Beatty is featured at the Bullfrog's heart. The Bullfrog Miner was published between April 8, 1905-July 1909.

Happy Hooligan Mine & Cave Rock Spring

GPS Coordinates Mine: 36°52'26.05"N 116°59'44.80"W
GPS Coordinates Spring: 36°52'10.75"N 117° 0'36.22"W

The Happy Hooligan Mine was one of the earliest prospects to be discovered in the now legendary Bullfrog Mining District. Three prospectors named McMann, Stockton and Wilson, first discovered the rich surface ore in May of 1905, along the hillside of what would go on to be known as "Hooligan Hill." Within a month of the discovery the prospectors were able to flip the mine to Curtis Mann and the Gorrill brothers, who formed the Happy Hooligan Mining Company.

It can only be assumed, but the company was likely named after the popular comic strip of the period by Frederick Burr Opper, called Happy Hooligan. The "Happy Hooligan" character was a well-meaning "hobo," that had plenty of bad luck, but wasn't willing let it get him down. His two brothers, "Gloomy Gus" and "Montmorency" were similar characters, however each with their own traits.

A month after the incorporation of the Happy Hooligan Mining Company, it was reported, "the mine consisted of an open surface cut and a discovery hole, where ore values of $22 to the ton had been uncovered." It was also reported that the mine owners intended to erect a mill at nearby Cave Rock Spring, which also served as

Scattered mining relics on the surface of the Happy Hooligan.

Open vertical shaft. NPS "Mine Hazard Area" warning sign.

the mine's camp. Because good news traveled like wildfire in these parts, soon the hills around the Happy Hooligan were crawling with miners, and the Happy Hooligan Mining Company had extensive competition.

As the summer of 1905 approached, all activities at the Happy Hooligan ceased. This was a common practice among mines in Death Valley Region. The temperatures were and still are known to reach the 110s and even at times well into the 120s.

As October rolled around, it was back to business as usual. It wasn't longer after, that the owners announced the discovery of ore found in the surface trenches ranging from $10 – $100 per ton. That called for the sinking of a shaft, and that they did! By November, the shaft had reached seventy feet, and Mann reported that the value was increasing with depth.

Around this same time, the town of Rhyolite was beginning to boom. It wouldn't be long before it was the largest city in Nevada, at least for a passing moment. The mine owners constructed a road linking the Happy Hooligan and Rhyolite.

By the end of 1905, the mine was reporting positive "that the ore vein was two feet wide and that the three shifts of miners employed on the property had sunk the inclined shaft to a depth of 120 feet." Despite that report, the government geologist which visited the mine reported, "The ore vein was rarely more than a few inches in width, and the future of the Happy Hooligan would depend entirely upon what conditions were uncovered as the shaft went deeper."

Up until this point, I don't believe that the Happy Hooligan owners had any intention of becoming swindlers, but future actions on their part could be looked at in any number of ways. After the report from the government geologist, Mann traveled to San Francisco and listed the Happy Hooligan on the city's stock exchange. Work continued on the mine, and in March of 1906 the company announced that it was ready to begin shipping their high-grade ore, and at the same time, they began running an advertising campaign for their stock in the Rhyolite Herald. Within three days of their first ad, they had sold 50,000 shares.

Finally in March the company began building a blacksmith shop and a boarding house. Up until this point the mine's camp was a half mile away at Cave Rock Spring, and their employees had actually been living in the caves at the spring. In April, the finishing touches were complete. The mine was now employing ten men, and had received a shipment of 500 ore sacks, to begin sacking the high-grade ore. By the end of May, the company announced that 500 sacks were full, and awaiting shipment.

In June the mine again went on hiatus for the summer, meanwhile the 500 sacks of high-grade ore never shipped. Share holders began to become annoyed and frustrated when in mid-September the mine had still not resumed operation. Stock prices began to fall, and at a share holder meeting, it was voted that work begin in the "immediate future."

Finally in October the company was able to regroup, and begin work once again. Stock holders began to feel comfortable again with the operation, despite the non-shipment of the high-grade ore, which the company reported ready to ship in May. Nevertheless, stock prices again rose.

A lot of excuses later, and finally over one year later, in March of 1908 the company disappeared from the stock exchange, having never shipped the 500 sacks of high-grade ore.

Visiting the site of the Happy Hooligan today, there isn't much remaining. The mines remain open, but appear unstable. There are at least two horizontal shafts, and a vertical shaft – which is all that I bothered to inspect. Scattered around the site of the mine are rusty cans, and discarded barrels – nothing much more.

The blacksmith shop, and boarding house are located a short distance from the mines. Neither building stands any longer, they have both been reduced to a pile of wood and nails. One of the buildings tin roofs remains surprisingly intact, discarded several feet from what was the structure.

A half a mile from the mine, I found the caves of Cave Rock Spring. The setting is picturesque, along an outcropping of stone on the eastern slopes of the Grapevine Mountains. While I found no flowing water, it is evident by the vibrant green vegetation that the spring still flows, but now underground. Along the stone outcroppings, there are a handful of caves, varying in size. Each of the caves containing extensive smoke damage, and large can dumps. Plenty of evidence of the miners that once worked the Happy Hooligan Mine.

Upon further inspection, I also noted several faint orange Native American pictographs outside of the largest of the caves.

By far the most interesting remains of the Happy Hooligan Mine, are those of Cave Rock Spring, showing the primitive manner in which these miners were forced to live.

Cave at Cave Spring. This cave was originally used by Native people, later by miners.

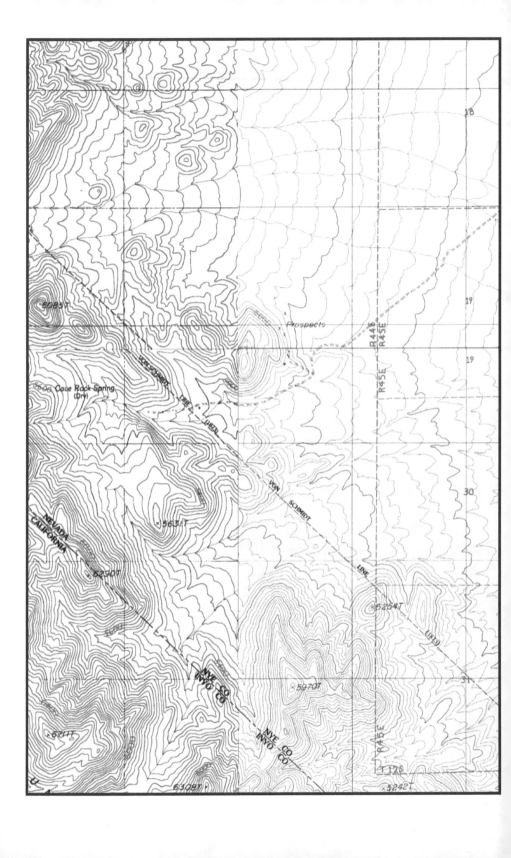

KLARE SPRING PETROGLYPHS (CALIFORNIA)

GPS Coordinates: 36°50'28.44"N 117° 5'26.54"W

Note: Klare Spring has been included in the Nevada Triange portion because access is limited to traveling Leadfield Rd. aka. Titus Canyon Road, which begins in Nevada.

This small petroglyph site in Titus Canyon, has been subjected to years of vandalism. So much so, that the original petroglyphs have become lost in the jumble of desecration.

The Native people who created these petroglyphs came to Klare Spring for both a water supply, and hunting. The spring attracted wildlife, like the native Bighorn Sheep. Petroglyphs at the site confirm this, a number of the designs represent sheep and water symbols. To this day Bighorn Sheep are known to frequent the area.

When visiting this petroglyph site, or any other, please do not add to any existing graffiti. New defacement will only lead to more restrictions, and less access to culturally significant sites.

Petroglyphs at Klare Spring.

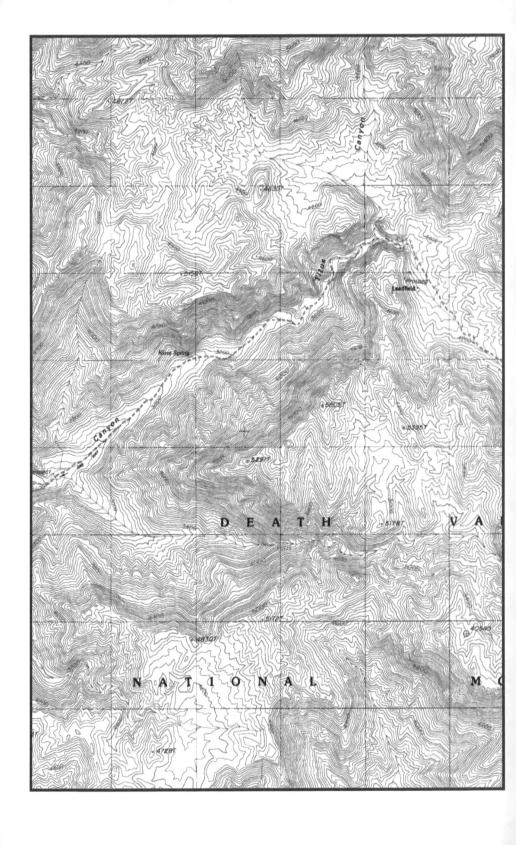

LEADFIELD (CALIFORNIA)

GPS Coordinates: 36°50'53.60"N 117° 3'35.47"W

Note: Leadfield has been included in the Nevada Triangle portion, because access is limited to traveling Leadfield Rd. aka. Titus Canyon Road, which begins in Nevada.

Leadfield, CA is located in the Grapevine mountains within the boundaries of Death Valley National Park. The story begins in 1905, twenty years before the town site would be plotted and officially be dubbed Leadfield. In the fall of that year two miners, W.H. Seaman and Curtis Durnford would stake 9 lead-copper claims which were the Romeo, Juliet, Sunset, Last Bit, Bustler, Humming Bird, Red Rube, Copper King, and Bobbie.

In December of 1905 W.H. Seaman, Curtis Durnford along with Clay Tallman (Rhyolite Attorney / Real Estate Promoter) formed the Death Valley Consolidated Mining Company. In May of 1906 the Death Valley Consolidated Mining Company was ready to begin shipping its ore to the smelters in Rhyolite. They soon realized that shipping the ore was not financially feasible, and they wouldn't be able to turn a profit. After just six shorts months the mines at the future site of Leadfield would be abandoned.

The future site of Leadfield stayed quiet for the better part of 18 years. In the spring of 1924 that would begin to change when three prospectors would make a claim on the mountaintop that overlooked the future Leadfield town site. The claim would be for Canyon Gate No. 1, the prospectors were Frank J. Metts, Lawrence Christiansen, and Ben Chambers. The three men would go on and locate many additional claims in the area.

At some point that same year the three men would be introduced to Jack Salsberry. Salsberry had owned the Carbonate lead mine in the Panamint Mountain Range, and backed a copper venture in Ubehebe in 1906. Salsberry would end up purchasing 22 claims from Metts, Christiansen, and Chambers. From those 22 claims, Salsberry would form four companies, Western Lead, Leadfield Carbonate, New Road, and Burr Welch. On August 17th 1925, Western Lead Mines (WLM) would file their incorporation papers in San Francisco.

Once WLM incorporated the word spread quickly about the claims in the Grapevine Mountains, and soon miners, business men, and swindlers began to flock to the area. In late November two-dozen people had arrived and began living in Leadfield. The town site was being surveyed, and 42-claims had been located. A road was beginning to be constructed up Titus Canyon. In December the road toward Beatty began construction. Lots in Leadfield began selling for between $150-$250.

In January of 1926 C.C. Julian arrived in Leadfield. Julian had recently dissolved his company Julian Petroleum as well the IRS was after him for $792,000 in back taxes, and he was brought up on mail fraud charges which would be dropped in exchange for hiring the federal investigator that was investigating him. On January 21st Julian would buy into WLM and become one of four partners, and later become President of WLM.

By the end of January it was estimated that 150-250 people where living in Leadfield. Telephone and telegraph wires had begun to be strung from Beatty, NV to Leadfield.

February 1st would see the beginning of Julian's famous advertising scheme to get unsuspecting investors to buy up WLM stocks. Julian's advertisement read more like newspaper articles, than advertisements. Headlines on Julian's ads read, "Death Valley and Her Hidden Treasure, That's my Baby Now", "Step on Her, Now", "Hot Dog", "Not Bad Business", "Come Up or Shut Up, That Choo Choo Leaves for Western Lead".

By late February, Leadfield was looking like a town. Hotels, mercantile stores, restaurants, a barbershop and bathhouse, saloons (though not called saloons at the time due to prohibition) all began to line the main street thought town (Chambers St.). Rumors ran amok of an airport, a 50-ton mill, and a 20-room hotel being built at Leadfield. None of which ever happened.

In March, Julian put together a weekend extravaganza in Leadfield, with the purpose of showing investors and potential investors the town and mines. That weekend in

The ruins of the Leadfield Post Office. Behind is the blacksmith shop.

March over 300 people arrived in Beatty via the Tonopah & Tidewater Railroad, and automobile. On Sunday a cavalcade made its way down the long and winding road to Leadfield. Visitors were sent on tours of various WLM audits, and were permitted to take sample sacks home with them (it is thought that whatever they found in their sacks was likely brought in from other locations, however that has never been proven).

The Monday after the extravaganza proved to be successful for Julian and WLM. The stock prices on the Los Angeles Stock Exchange for WLM soared to $3.30 a share. That was however short-lived as the following day it had leaked that the California Corporate Commission was investigating Julian and WLM. Trading prices dropped to $1.88. On Wednesday the California Corporate Commission launched their attack on WLM, and by Thursday the Los Angeles Stock Exchange had to set up barricades to keep angry WLM investors at bay as prices for WLM stock dropped to $.90, and closed at $1.75. Friday WLM fell to $1.33, and closed at $1.50.

WLM wasn't the only mining company in town, but little had success in Leadfield. A mill nor ore bins had ever been erected at Leadfield, despite many promises. Julian at one point even advertised that steam boats would eventually come up the Amargosa River, and be able to dock near Leadfield. Anyone that has ever seen the Amargosa River knows that this is not possible as majority of the Amargosa flows underground, and the parts that are above ground you'd have a hard time putting any boat on, much less a steam boat.

Blacksmith shop.

April 5th began the California Corporate Commission hearings on Julian and WLM. The hearings would last until April 27th, at which time the state would rule again Julian and WLM. Despite the ruling business would continue as usual for WLM until May 27th when the Chief Deputy Corporate Commissioner handed down the decision to stop the sale of WLM stocks in California once and for all. That same day WLM was stricken from the Los Angeles Stock Market. While this was a huge blow to Julian and WLM, it didn't slow him down.

WLM was still listed on the Reno Stock Exchange, but was listed at $.65, not even half of the original asking price on the Los Angeles Stock Exchange. Julian continued to try to keep things going, accumulating a large portion of the low-priced WLM stock. Not everyone had given up on Julian yet, as he still had a good number of prospectors, townspeople, and even some investors behind him.

Other mining companies would come and go in Leadfield, none of them would ever ship any ore including Julian's WLM. In August Leadfield's post office would officially open. 200 people at the time would receive their mail in Leadfield. The post office would stay open until February of the following year, when only one person was left to receive mail in Leadfield.

Ruins of the Leadfield Hotel in 1939. Photograph by Edward Weston
Collection Center for Creative Photography © 1981 Center for Creative Photography, Arizona Board of Regents

As for Julian, he went on to be indicted for mail fraud in 1931. That same year he was also arrested for kidnapping and threatening a former employee. In 1932 he would file for bankruptcy claiming $3,057,430.53 in liabilities and no assets. In 1933 he jumped bail on the mail fraud charges and flee to Canada. On March 23rd, 1934 Julian was found dead in a Shanghai, China hotel from a fatal dose of amytal.

At the Leadfield town site today you will find a few still standing metal buildings, dug outs that had once been used for housing, the concrete slab from the power plant, stone walls, wooden floor boards, as well as many rusty cans and a rusted automobile frame. All of the mine entrances have been blocked off by the Park Service. The current road driven through the town-site is the same road that was once the main street through town (Chambers Street).

The Leadfield Pioneer Club in 1925. The Leadfield Hotel sign didn't belong on this building, and was likely moved there after the town was abandoned.

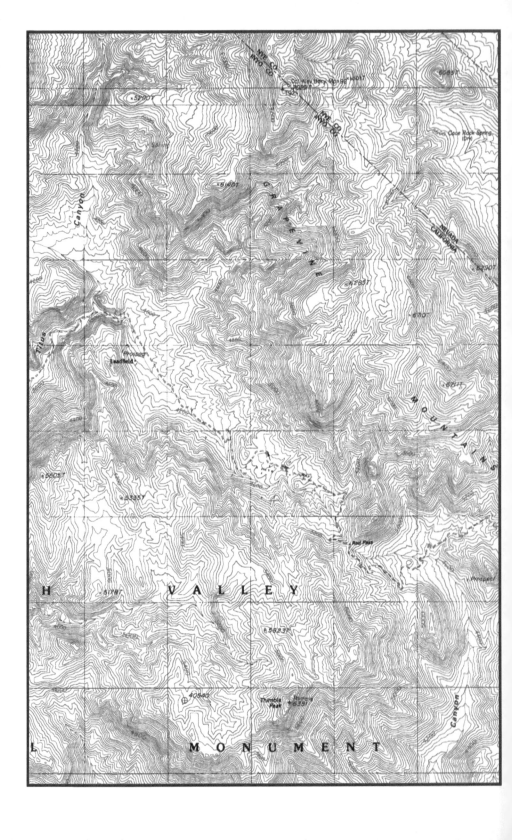

PHINNEY MINE

GPS Coordinates: 36°57'32.58"N 117° 6'28.41"W

When one thinks of Death Valley National Park the image of pine trees, and forest doesn't usually enter one's mind. Rather stark landscapes, brutal heat, and rocks, lots of rocks are what is imagined. This isn't always the case however, many of the high peeks in Death Valley National Park are blanketed in forest, and even receive a fair amount of powdery white snow during the winter months. The Phinney Mine is one of such places, located in Phinney Canyon at 6,775 feet in the Grapevine Mountains, part of the "Nevada Triangle."

The Phinney Mine sprang to life during the depression era in the 1930's as a two man mining operation, with Charles E. and F. C. Phinney, both from Beatty, NV as the proprietors. The two men worked the mine through 1938, shipping a total of fifty ounces of ore, amounting to about $850. Seeing no profitability they abandoned the mine. Charles Phinney and his wife Florence settled in the nearby community of Beatty, NV, where Charles passed in 1951 (NPS has his death as 1952, however cemetery records indicate 1951).

The Phinney Mine can be accessed via a short hike up a side canyon located at 36°57'26.80"N 117° 6'21.70"W. At the mouth of this canyon there is significant traces of a mining camp, including an old metal water tank, advertising "Fotos of Death Valley." Further up the canyon are the ruins of the mine, including a large can dump, and a collapsed cabin on the side of a ravine. There are two adits, one is partially collapsed at the entrance, while the other remains stable and still contains the ore cart tracks.

Cabin at Phinney Mine - 1978. NPS photo.

To some the Phinney Mine may come across as insignificant, however I find that it is a perfect example of depression era mining. It showcases the struggle of two men that worked hard with minimal supplies, for very little in return. They did this in an environment that was harsh and life threatening, something that we wouldn't see in today's society of technology and cushy lifestyles.

What remains of the Phinney Mine cabin today.

Entrance to one of the mine adits.

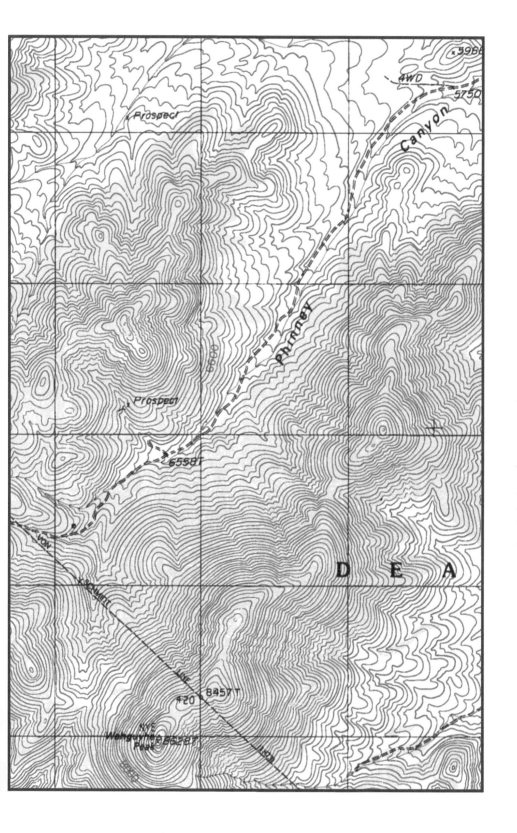

SARCOBATUS SPRING SHELTER

GPS Coordinates: 36°58'9.37"N 116°59'45.75"W

Traipsing around the backcountry of Death Valley National Park can be a lot of fun, it is such a vast area that one never knows what hidden gem they may encounter. The key is to be alert to anything and everything that may look out-of-place or unusual.

On a recent trip I had focused on investigating the springs that are located in the Nevada Triangle of the park. Why springs, you ask? Springs have been a natural gathering point for humans since their inception, as well as all other animal species. In most cases where you find a spring you will find traces of past habitation, whether it be Native American villages or "rock art," or ranches, homesteads, or even mining ruins from early white settlers.

Between Phinney Canyon and Currie Well I had noted an unnamed spring on an old topo map of the area. I was unable to locate any further information, but I figured it was still a worthwhile stop to investigate, even it didn't amount to anything more than a trickle seeping out of the ground. Just shy of reaching the spring a wall of stones on a nearby hillside caught my eye. Being the good little adventurer that I strive to be, I decided to check it out.

Walking up the hill I immediately began to find rusty cans, a good sign that early settlers had utilized the area, but not only did I find rusty cans, I also found lithic scatters. Lithic scatters is a fancy way of saying prehistoric garbage, or in other words the chipped leftover stone from flint knapping. Finding both of these elements heightened my curiosity about the stone wall that was making my way toward.

Approaching the stone wall, I realized that it was much more than just a wall. The wall was actually built up along-side a natural rock shelter. Stashed inside was an assortment of

The shelter at "Sarcobatus Spring"

random rusty goodies, and old weathered wood. A tin cup hung from a rust covered wire. This shelter obviously had a past to it, only it remains historically undocumented. Looking a little closer at the walls of the shelter, orange pigment caught my eye. Sure enough, there were also Native American pictographs in the shelter. Further examining of the shelter revealed more lithic scatter, like those that I had found near the bottom of the hill.

To me I find it very interesting the way that an early settler (probably a miner) utilized the space that an earlier people had once used, and you can visibly see the difference in lifestyle and culture. This is not the first time that I have seen this, and I'm sure that it won't be the last time either.

Just a short distance from the shelter the spring is located, essentially a hole in the earth with water filling it. Hundreds if not thousands of animal prints are in abundance in the mud surrounding it. To the people who once used the shelter, this spring was a life source. Not only would it have provided them with water to drink, but also animals to eat.

"Sarcobatus Spring"

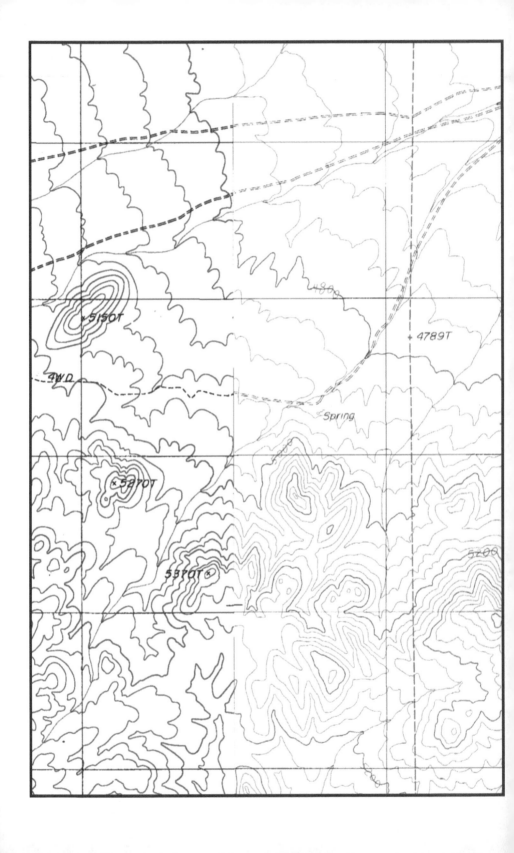

STROZZI RANCH

GPS Coordinates: 36°56'30.71"N 117° 4'28.19"W

One place in Death Valley where I have done little to no previous research or exploring is the "Nevada Triangle," a 300,000-acre parcel of land within the National Park which falls in the Silver State. I've had no excuse for ignoring it up until this point, other than having other places of interest take precedence over it. "The Triangle" is a rather remote portion of the park, no major roads enter it, and it is totally disconnected from the main valley – or even California in general, via road. On a recent excursion to Death Valley, I finally dedicated two days to get out there and see what Death Valley had to offer in it's "triangle".

I went armed with only my trusty Death Valley National Geographic Trails Illustrated Map, and no previous research. I wanted an element of surprise, and no expectations. I spent the first day exploring in Phinney Canyon, which travels high into the woodlands of the Grapevine Mountains. From Phinney Canyon, I traveled over to Brier Spring, and Currie Well – not much is actually listed on the map for this region, but between these places, and other hidden gems along the way, there are several interesting sites.

I was en route to Brier Springs, expecting to find a small stream with a trickle of water. Several rock shelters along the road piqued my interest, and warranted investigation for the possibilities of their being Native American rock art (Pictographs & Petroglyphs). While there was no rock art, there was several telling signs that the shelters had been occupied at one point, however not by Native Americans, but rather by miners. That is not to say that Native people had not occupied the shelters prior to the miners, but any surface evidence was not present. Instead the surface elements present were that of rusty discarded cans.

From the shelters I continued on down the dusty dirt road, while the sage brush which filled the landscape gently rattled in the wind. A fork in the road soon presented itself, and I opted for the right hand path. It abruptly came to an end at an old rustic fence, pieced together using rotting branches from an assortment of trees, and metal wire.

What the heck is this I asked myself? Excited, I jumped out of the Jeep to investigate closer. Behind the fence was a massive rock shelter with extensive amount of smoke damage, and a bright green patch of grass. A seep must protrude from somewhere from within the shelter, as the grassy patch seemed moist, and a high concentration of honey bees enjoyed harassing me. The fence was rustic, and appealing to the eye. It was old, and obviously well made at the time of its construction. But why?

Returning to my vehicle, I figured that I would find the answer later – later would come just moments later as I turned back onto the road in which I came, returning to the fork, and continuing on up toward Brier Springs. Going around a singular bend, I saw a sight that I hadn't expected, a half-dozen charming, yet rustic buildings. In a singular moment, my day was made. Abandoned buildings are on my favorite subjects to pho

Dug-out style building at Strozzi Ranch.

Workshop at Strozzi Ranch.

tograph, and explore around.

Caesar Strozzi, an immigrant from Switzerland had built this homestead in 1931. Strozzi and his wife Mary utilized the homestead as a seasonal ranch, spending the summers here raising his cattle, goats, and chickens. When Strozzi was not at the homestead, he resided in the nearby town of Beatty.

Strozzi constructed several structures on the homestead including a small ranch house, blacksmith shop, a chicken house, and various other work shops. Water was piped in from Brier Springs, situated just a quarter of a mile up the hill. Brier Spring also allowed for the opportunity to plant crops, a few peach trees are still situated near the spring itself.

Strozzi utilized the homestead from 1931 until 1947. He died in Beatty, NV in 1953, and is buried at the Desert Hill Cemetery.

These rustic buildings which have stood for nearly 85 years, are a glimpse into a time when people worked hard, they broke their back for whatever they had. Electricity was nonexistent (unless they had generator) in a remote place like this, and down time was likely spent reading a book, tinkering in the shop, or reminiscing about "the good ole' days". Time sure wasn't wasted talking about the latest music sensation, tv shows, and certainly not the latest cat meme.

Ranch house and additional outbuildings at Strozzi Ranch.

Poking around the structures reveals bits and pieces of the life of Caesar and Mary, as small pieces of their lives still remain. In the main house, boxes from Pacific Coast Biscuit Co., and Sears Roebuck wallpaper the small living quarters. In the kitchen lids from jars of Lady's Choice, and Best Foods. An old stove sits rusting out front. In the workshops, there are rusty tools, and various odds and ends which fill the hand-made shelves.

This is an amazing place, a place worth preservation. Unfortunately the NPS seems to disagree. In their Inventory of Historic Resources, it is said of Strozzi Ranch, "The attempt has no historical importance, and the buildings at the ranch do not deserve preservation." While this report is severely dated (1981), lets hope that since the ranch has now well passed the 50 year mark, they are now seeing things differently, and Strozzi Ranch will survive for as long as the elements allow it.

Ceasar Strozzi (circa 1940)

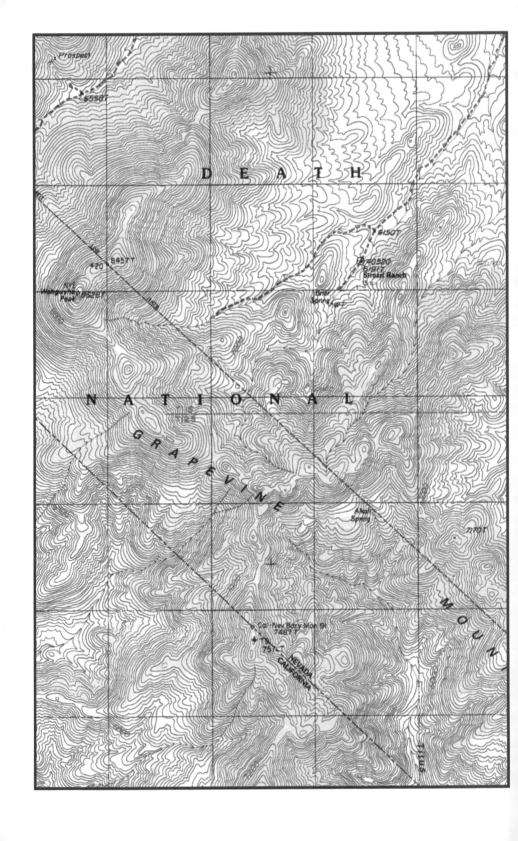

"The desert is the theater of the human struggle of searching for God."

-Jan Majernik

Northern Death Valley

CRATER MINE

GPS Coordinates: 37°12'42.01"N 117°41'18.93"W

The area surrounding the Crater Mine contains the largest deposit of sulfur west of the Mississippi River, created by a hydrothermal reaction to the vapor phase of a hot spring system feeding up through limestones and dolomites. The sulfur deposits were discovered in 1917, but little action took place until around 1929.

The Crater-El Capitan Mining District consisted of a small number of mines. The largest of those workings was the Crater Group, which even supported a small company town, aptly named Crater. Crater never grew into anything more than a "one horse town," reaching its peak of thirty-six people in 1931.

The Crater Mine was active until 1953, when a sulfur-dust explosion blew-up the mill site. Some small scale mining took place between 1957 and 1986. In the 1990's a large scale mining operation moved in, destroying what had remained of the former town of Crater, and much of the early mining equipment.

When Death Valley graduated from National Monument to National Park in 1994, and additional land added to the National Park Service protection, Crater was not included because of its status as private land. Despite its current state of abandonment the Crater Mine remains private property. Today, Crater consists of mostly abandoned machinery from the later era of mining.

Late era mining equipment is all that remains at the Crater Mine.

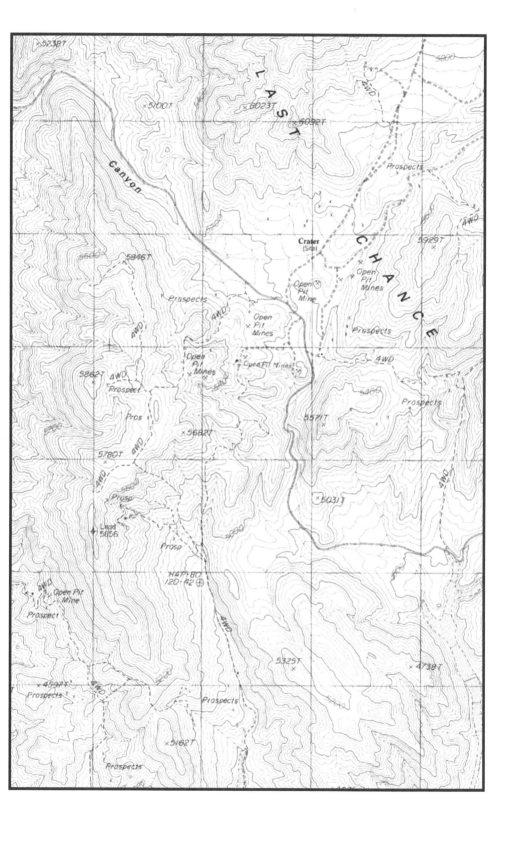

EUREKA VALLEY OVERLOOK

GPS Coordinates: 37°11'55.76"N 117°42'23.46"W

I've come to learn that everyone enjoys a good overlook, and this particular overlook is one that I've rarely seen Eurerka Valley photographed from. To the south it provides stunning views of the Eureka Dunes, Last Chance Mountains, Saline Range, and the opening of Dedeckera Canyon. To the northwest, the wide open valley, Big Pine Road, and in the distance the Inyo Mountains meeting the Saline Range.

The road to the overlook is not included on any maps, however it is not signed closed. Just west of the Crater Sulfur Mine take the unmaintained road leading southwest. This road will lead up a series of washes to the overlook. 4x4 is recommenced.

Looking south out over the Eureka Dunes, Last Chance Mountains, Saline Range, and the opening of Dedeckera Canyon.

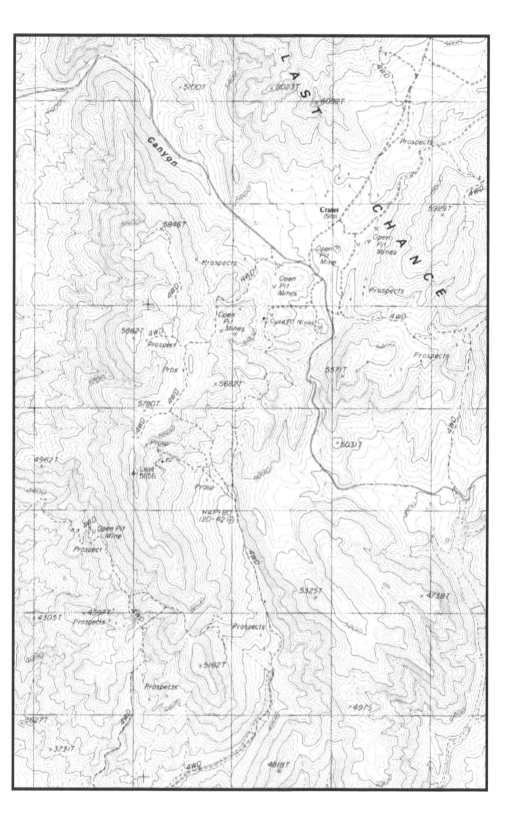

Marble Bath

GPS Coordinates: 36°58'11.45"N 117°38'9.13"W

In 1994 Death Valley National Park was upgraded from National Monument to National Park, at that same time the National Park Service expanded the boundaries to include additional lands. Included in that land was an area called Steel Pass, which connects Eureka Valley with Saline Valley. Much to the confusion of many, for the longest time USGS maps had marked this area as "Marble Bath."

Before the park service took over the land, Wendel Moyer, a desert rat that had visited the area for several years decided that "Marble Bath" was actually in need of a bath tub filled with marbles. Moyer and several of his friends rounded up an old claw-tooth bath rub, and boxes of marbles. They installed the tub in the location that was identified as "Marble Bath" on the maps.

Moyer's "Marble Bath" remains where he installed, and has become a popular stop for people traveling between the valleys.

As it turns out the "Marble Bath" indicated on USGS maps is a small pool on the east side of the road. The pool is now usually empty of water, which is what likely caused the confusion.

A bath tub filled with marbles along Steel Pass.

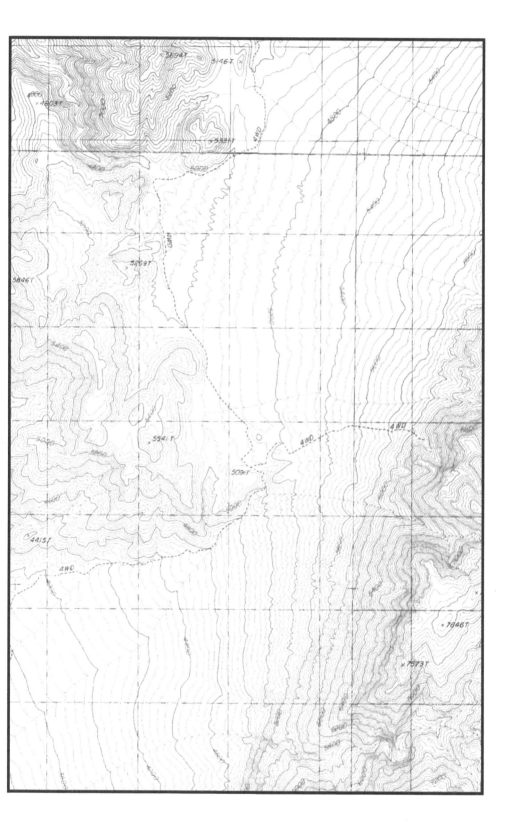

MESQUITE SPRINGS PETROGLYPHS

GPS Coordinates: 36°57'8.12"N 117°22'46.20"W

Mesquite Springs was once a village site to the Shoshone people. Today it serves as a campground to visitors of Death Valley National Park. Less than a mile from the campground, on the alluvial fan above the springs there are several boulders containing petroglyphs. These petroglyphs are believed to be between 2,000 - 3,000 years old, they are carved into the desert varnish on the basalt rock.

Panel of petroglyphs at Mesquite Springs.

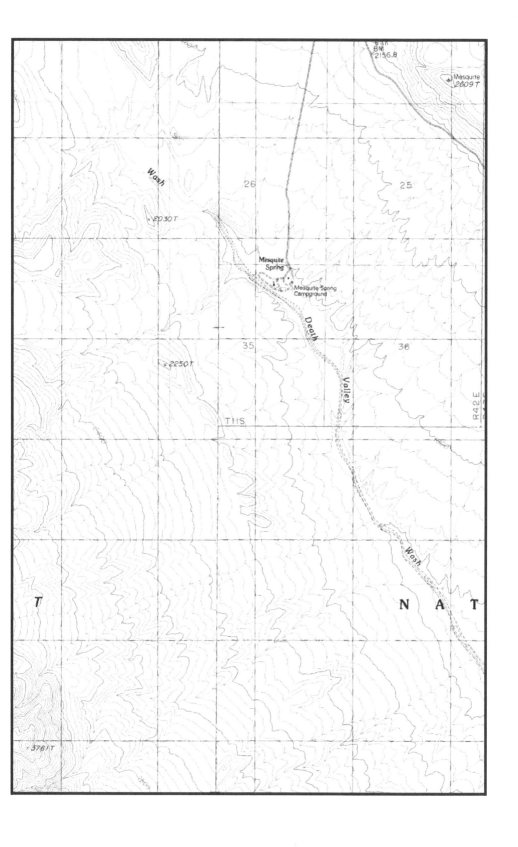

"Love me or hate me,
the desert seems to say,
this is what I am and
this is what I shall remain."

-Joseph Wood Krutch

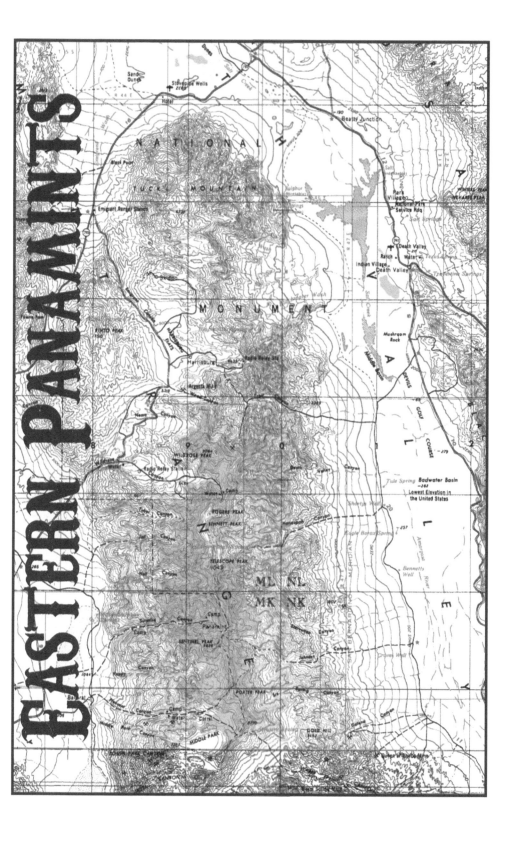

Emigrant Canyon Petroglyphs

GPS Coordinates: 36°23'47.16"N 117° 9'34.59"W

Emigrant Canyon is one of those canyons that has many landscape, historic, and prehistoric features. The road leading through the canyon, which also bares its name, begins in Death Valley, off of Highway 190, near Emigrant Campground and the abandoned Emigrant Ranger Station. The road travels from desolate desert, through rocky canyon, to rolling hills, and eventually a forest of pinyon pine – once the road becomes Charcoal Kiln Road. The temperature from point A to point B can vary 20-30 degrees, depending on the season.

Emigrant Canyon received its name, because it was believed that members of the pioneering 49er party had used this canyon as an escape route from Death Valley. While it is possible, it is now more widely speculated that they had utilized canyons or passes further to the west, including the neighboring Jayhawker Canyon. In the late 1800s the canyon was used as a wagon wheel route, connecting the various mining camps and communities along its way.

Today a shadow of many of these camps and communities exist, whether it be Skidoo, Harrisburg, Wildrose, or any of the other small camps in the region. In the 1970's, the National Park Service in Death Valley, had hired a superintendent that was hell bent on the removal of historic structures. That is why there is little remaining of these places today.

Petroglyphs in Emigrant Canyon.

Before the "whites" came to the region, Emigrant Canyon provided one of several routes from the valley floor to the high reaches of the Panamint Mountains for the Timbisha Shoshone. The Timbisha Shoshone resided in the Death Valley area for possibly thousands of years, and they continue to do so today. These Native peoples resided in both the mountain ranges, and stark valleys below, varying based on the time of the year.

The petroglyphs that have been carved into the limestone cliff face, are not far from the site of Emigrant Springs – likely the reason for their creation at this location. For those unaware, petroglyphs are often found near the source of springs, or places that water was known to collect. This could be for a number of reasons, but most speculate that it had to do with the abundant amount of wildlife that would frequent these location. In reality we don't really know why, and most speculation is just educated guesses.

The Emigrant Canyon petroglyphs consist of images that are similar to others in the region. A number of zoomorphic images, depicting bighorn sheep; along with anthropomorphic, or human looking designs. There are also a significant amount of abstract designs, in the form of chains, squiggles, circles, and meandering lines.

One particular anthropomorphic design caught my attention, it is located high on a shelf, above the main panel. The petroglyph depicts five-human figures with their hands in the air, and their legs in a wide stance. The figures are no larger than two inches. This may very well depict a ritual, or a dance – but again, this is speculation.

Bighorn sheep petroglyphs in Emigrant Canyon.

As well as the dozens of petroglyphs, there is a singular pictograph design, consisting of four orange lines. It is likely that at one time there were others, but years of exposure to the elements may have completely erased them.

Overall this is a very enjoyable site, it is easy to access, and just a couple of hundred feet from the roadway. Next time you drive through Emigrant Canyon, slow down and you may just find yourself a treat.

Five anthropomorphic figures.

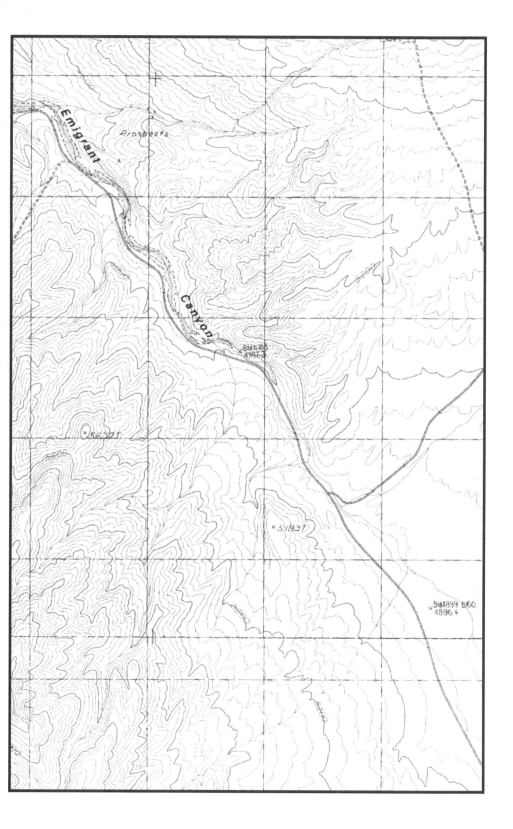

GRAVES OF FRANK SHORTY HARRIS & JAMES DAYTON

GPS Coordinates: 36°12'27.25"N 116°52'12.01"W

The graves of Frank "Shorty" Harris and James Dayton are situated along West Side Road between the turn offs for Hanaupah and Johnson Canyons. It was at this location that James Dayton died in July of 1898, while crossing Death Valley on his way to the town of Daggett.

Dayton was a caretaker for Pacific Coast Borax Company at Furnace Creek. He had been en-route to Daggett to pick-up supplies for the company, but never made it. Nearly a month later word reached back to Furnace Creek, and a search party began the hunt for Dayton. Only twenty miles from where he departed, they found Dayton's body along with the lifeless bodies of his six-horse team. The only survivor was his pet dog. It is speculated the Dayton died of an illness that he had come down with before the trip, or of a heat related illness. The wagon which he was pulling contained sufficient amounts of both food and water, so dehydration likely didn't play a roll. Dayton was buried on the site of his death. His eulogy read, "Well Jimmie, you lived in the heat and you died in the heat, and after what you've been through, I guess you ought to be comfortable in hell." (writers note: I can only hope that something so kind is said about me upon my death.)

The graves of Frank Shorty Harris & James Dayton

Frank "Shorty" Harris was the quintessential example of a Death Valley prospector. It was often said that "Shorty" had the ability to "smell gold," because of his keen ability to discover good claims. Despite his ability, and being responsible for discovering the areas largest producer, the Bullfrog Mining District, "Shorty" never actually owned or operated a mining operation. "Shorty" preferred to drink away what little profits he would make from selling a claim. Once funds would deplete, he would again begin the search for good gold-bearing ground.

"Shorty" prospected for most of his adult life, first in Colorado, Arizona and Idaho. A majority of his prospector years were however spent in the Death Valley region. He died in 1934 at the age of 78, at his cabin in Big Pine. He requested to be buried beside his old friend James Dayton in Death Valley, with his tombstone reading, "Here lies Shorty Harris, a single blanket jackass prospector – 1856-1934."

The grave of James Dayton in the 1930's.

From left to right: "Death Valley "Scotty," Frank "Shorty" Harris

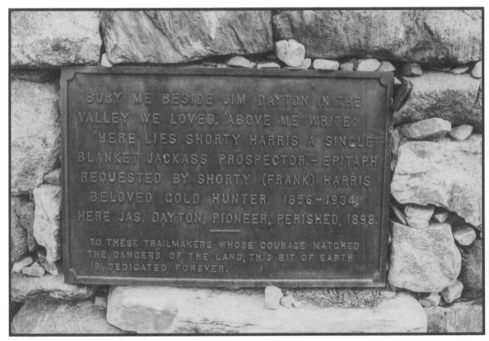

Memorial for Frank "Shorty" Harris.

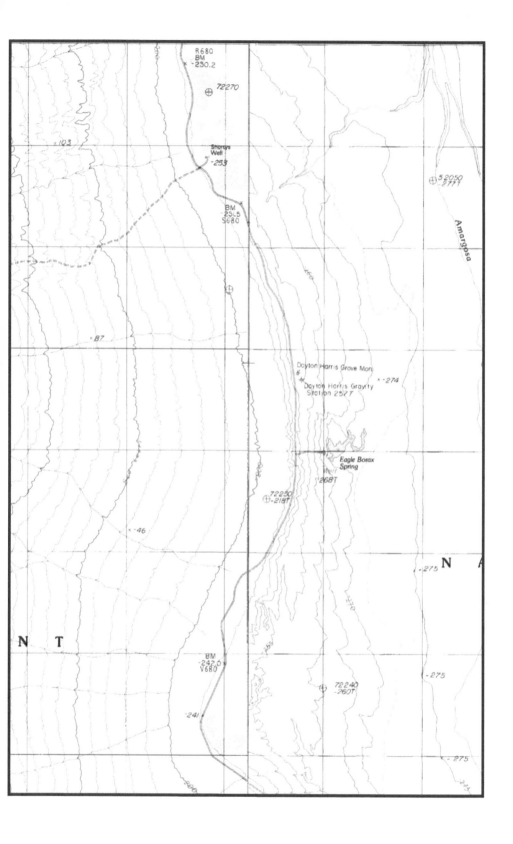

HUNGRY BILL S RANCH & JOHNSON CANYON

GPS Coordinates: 36° 5'33.02"N 117° 1'50.39"W

Johnson Canyon Road runs from the floor of Death Valley and travels several miles up an alluvial before entering the confines of Johnson Canyon, and finally to Wilson Spring. The length of the 4×4 trail is roughly 10 miles, and at the time of this writing, it doesn't pose many difficulties with the exception of a couple of rocky spots. Remember however that road conditions in these areas can change quickly, one cloudburst can alter the landscape significantly. It took just a little over an hour to travel the duration of the road.

Once at Wilson Spring, it is time to set off on foot. I was impressed with the beauty of the oasis which included a small grove of Cottonwood Trees, surrounded by vibrant green desert scrub, and a small perennial stream. A well-groomed trail left the oasis, and traveled up the canyon following the path of the spring. Several times early in the hike, the spring is crossed, but fellow hikers have made these crossing as friendly as possible, by placing stepping-stones across the slick and muddy spring.

Not far up canyon from the oasis, there are the ruins of a Spanish arrastra. The trail runs directly past it, but it can be easily missed among the assortment of brush that has grown up around the very primitive mining mill. The sidewalls and base of the arrastra remain in tact, however the drag stone, which would have been used to crush the ore is missing. Further up the canyon, the ruins of a second arrastra lay in a state of unrecognizable ruin, with a third located near the actual ranch site.

A half a mile or so into the hike the canyon quickly narrows and becomes overgrown with dense vegetation, the trail leaves the floor of the canyon and ascends high above on the eastern wall. Elevation is gained quickly, but again the trail is well maintained. Once hiking along the ridge, I caught my first glimpse of the large stone walls, that I had heard so much about. A large retaining wall slithers its way from the trail down 200 feet to the canyon bottom. This wall is no joke, a considerable amount of time and effort was put into building something of this magnitude.

Roughly a quarter of a mile past the behemoth stone wall, the trail comes to an abrupt end, with a good 40 feet between you and the floor of the canyon. This is the most technical part of the hike, and potentially could cause some puckering to anyone not accustom with maneuvering their way down a cliff face.

Once in the canyon below, another magnificent stone walls sits among the overgrown desert oasis. While not near as impressive as the 200 footer, it is still a testament to the skills that went into building it. Here is also where the trail picks back up; crosses the canyon, and ascends the western wall of the canyon. I of course didn't notice that the trail picked back up, and forged my way through the dense vegetation. The going was rough, reminding me a bit of a scaled back Beverage Canyon (in the Inyo Mountains). I soon found myself with the option of trudging through a swampy marsh, or heading up the western canyon wall. I decided on the wall of the canyon, in which I would find the trail which I should have followed all along.

The trail led me through a patch of gnarly, asshole shrubs with big and pointy spines. I was lucky, and didn't leave any flesh or blood behind – but there were a few close calls. Finally past the garden of puncture wounds, I entered the lower portion of Hungry Bill's Ranch. The ruins again consist of substantial well-built stone walls, and the first trees of the old fruit orchard. One has to wonder where the time was found to do anything but build stone walls – and why so many?

Exploring the ranch site was interesting, consisting of some period rusty relics, fruit tree orchards (which still produce fruit), smoke damaged caves, and even more stone walls. The highlight of the journey wasn't so much the ruins, but rather the gorgeous canyon filled with lush springs, rock formations, and the overwhelmingly positive feeling of being a lone in the remote desert/mountainous landscape.

You are probably wondering at this point, who was this Hungry Bill character, and what is the story with this remote ranch…

The earliest history on the ranch, is that it was built and the orchard planted by William Johnson in 1873. As you might have guessed the canyon is named after this bloke.

Ruins of a spanish arrastra in Johnson Canyon.

Johnson Canyon

Johnson would peddle his wares to the miners in Panamint City, until it went bust in 1876. Johnson would quickly move on, and leave the Death Valley area.

Hungry Bill was a full-blooded Shoshone Indian, he lived and ranched at this site as early as 1880; having been deeded the ranch after Johnson abandoned it, for his payment as a scout in the Modoc Wars. He was born around 1839, and married a full-blooded Shoshone woman named, Ce-un-ba-hobe. Together they would raise two sons, and two daughters.

Hungry Bill received his name from miners, because of his habit of entering mining camps to beg for food. Bill and his brother Panamint Tom had quiet the reputation in their younger years, leading horse-stealing raids into Los Angeles. Both Bill and Tom would settle down in their later years, and helped in the construction of roads across the Death Valley salt flats.

Hungry Bill died in 1919 of the flu and his wife passed away three years later.

Stone wall ruins at Hungry Bill's Ranch.

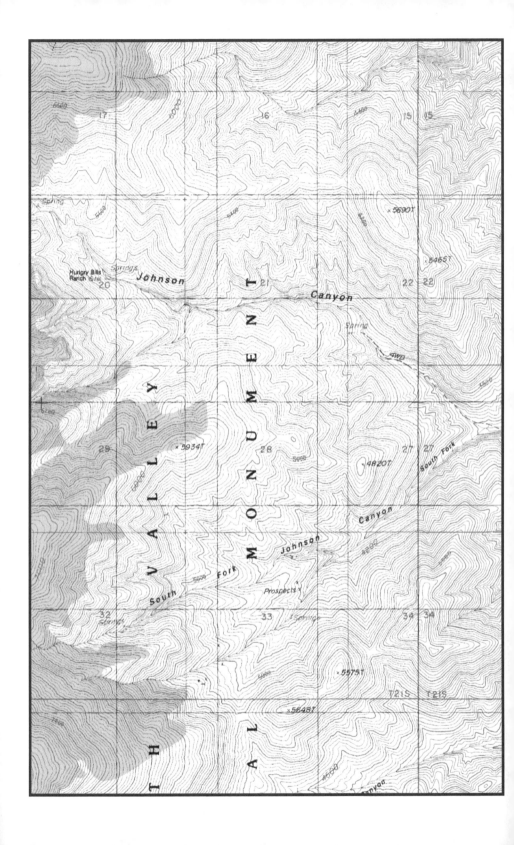

QUEEN OF SHEBA MINE

GPS Coordinates: 35°59'58.68"N 116°53'6.80"W

If you have spent any amount of time reading or researching about the thousands of mines in the vicinity of Death Valley, you are likely aware that few amounted to much more than hype. If it wasn't hype, it was discovered that the cost of transporting the ore from the mines was too costly, resulting in little or no profit for mine owners. Despite these facts, miners and prospectors flocked to the Death Valley vicinity in search of riches – hoping to be more successful than their predecessors. In a rare occurrence success would be had, the Carbonite (also known as Carbonate) and Queen of Sheba proved to be one of those successes, but not without a lot of hard work.

In the blistering summer of 1907, Clarence E. Eddy was exploring the southwestern slopes of the Panamint Mountains, when he found a large galena outcrop. No sooner than he began the development process, word of his strike had spread. Other prospectors came calling, and it wasn't long before Frank Stockton and a mining engineer named Chester A. Pray, located what would become known as the Carbonite Mine. Unfortunately for Eddy, his original "find" never amounted to anything, with the exception of credit for being the original locator of the outcrop.

To expand a little further on Clarence E. Eddy, he was not so much your typical prospector. He was known by his fellow prospectors and the media, as the poet-prospector. Eddy had played the roll of a newspaper editor, miner/prospector, author, and poet. His works include, The Pinnacle of Parnassus (1902), The House of Hell: A Ballad of Blackfoot (1909), The Burros Bray (1922), and Ballads of Heaven and Hell (1923). Overall his mining endeavors in Death Valley never amount too much, making him more of a poet than a miner/prospector. However without his experiences, he likely would not have written poetry that rang so true to the west.

After Stockton and Prey located the Carbonite, two fellows by the names of Jack Salsberry and Ed Chafey took interest in the mine. They formed the Carbonate Lead Mines Company of Death Valley. Due to their interest, a small camp sprung up below the mine, it was also named Carbonite. The usual problem of transportation was quickly resolved by Salsberry, in the form of a wagon road from Salt Wells to the eastern side of the Black Mountains (today we continue to use this route – "Salsbury Pass"). The wagon would haul the ore across Death Valley, and over the Amargosa Mountains. From there the ore would be transferred to a tractor, which would haul the ore the final sixteen miles to the Tonopah and Tidewater Railroad station at Zabriskie.

Despite the hard work of building a road, as well securing the animals to haul the wagon, by 1913 only two rail cars of ore had been shipped out of Carbonite. The summer months were rough, and the miners had a tendency to sleep in the mines to escape the heat of the valley. Workers at the Carbonite had documented temperatures reaching up to 164 degrees in the shade (despite the official highest temperature in the world of 134 degrees, having been records just a short distance away that same year).

That winter, CLMC was able to expand their number of workers, and by February of 1914, the camp was being referred to as the "latest sensation of the western mining world." The large deposits of lead, silver, gold, and copper that were being found were mighty impressive. Lead and silver ore values supposedly as high as two million dollars.

CLMC's success was beginning to become apparent, when just a few short months later they ditched the mules for sixteen large trucks. The trucks were able to drive direct from Carbonite to Zabriskie, and deliver one rail car full of ore per day. They were averaging between $57.50 to $75.00 per ton.

Between 1915 to 1918, the Carbonite had produced 11,000 tons of lead and silver ore. However in 1920, the mine was listed as inactive – but was likely operated on and off between then and 1923.

In 1923 there was a rather confusing shift of deeds, but in the end, the New Sutherland Divide Mining Company took control. They leased the property to U.S. Smelting, Refining & Mining Company. Work began again on the Carbonite Mine, and also, the Queen of Sheba was born.

Miner's cabin at the Queen of Sheba Mine.

Report Twenty of the State Mineralogist Concerning Mining in California and the Activities of the State Mining Bureau reported, "6,500 tons of sorted ore that had been shipped to the Salt Lake City smelter averaged 40% lead and 20 ozs. silver per ton. At the prices later reached for lead in 1926, this amount of ore could have grossed over $500,000."

In the February 27th, 1926 edition of the Inyo Independent, it was stated that the Queen of Sheba was "the largest body of proved commercial-grade ore in the Death Valley region". Despite that news, U.S. Smelting, Refining & Mining Company surrendered their lease of the operation.

Over the course of the next thirty-five years many mining companies came and went, with the final lessee, a Mr. Ray Bennett in 1961.

Total production of the Queen of Sheba has reportedly been 16,000 tons of crude ore yielding 5,000,000 lbs. of lead, 100,000 ozs. of silver, 1,500 ozs. of gold, and 146,000 lbs. of copper. Ore from the mine has averaged 15.5% lead, .5% copper, 6.3 ozs. of silver, and .09 oz. of gold per ton.

Today, one may visit the ruins of the Queen of Sheba and Carbonite, via a four-mile dirt road that leads off of the valley floor, from West Side Road. The road itself is rough at times, and crosses several washed out areas. High clearance, and four-wheel drive are recommended.

Ore bin at Queen of Sheba Mine

Most of the significant ruins are to be found at the site of the Queen of Sheba. Two shacks, which are believed to have been from the 1940's or even the 1930's remain standing near the site of the mill. Two ore bins, several pieces of large rusted mining equipment, as well as concrete slabs, make up what is remaining of the mill. At the site of the mine itself, a picturesque ore chute extends from the cut in the mountain above.

The site of the camp or town of Carbonite has long been lost, its exact location remains a mystery.

A depilated ore chute leaves the mouth of the mine adit.

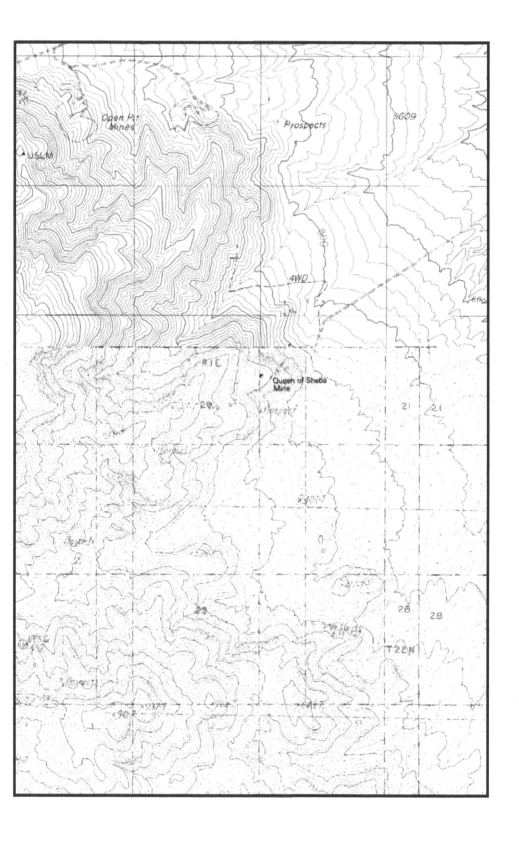

Tucki Mine

GPS Coordinates: 36°27'9.11"N 117° 5'26.28"W

The Tucki Mine is tucked away on the southwest flank of Tucki Mountain, part of the Panamint Mountain Range. It is reached via Tucki Mine Road, a ten-mile stretch of dirt road, which leaves the pavement 1.7 miles up Wildrose Road from Emigrant Junction. The road travels up a section of Telephone Canyon, before splitting off into a side canyon.

The natural beauty of the canyon, the peaks, and the vast views of the valley are the show stealer here. The mine ruins pale in comparison to the breathtaking beauty of the natural world that surround it. There are several vantages that allow for optimal viewing of Death Valley. Roughly 1.25 miles before the Tucki Mine ruins, a spur road travels north up the ridge. Follow this road for .75 miles to the wilderness boundary for an intense overview of the valley, and the Funeral Mountains. For those that are interested you can continue to hike this road for 1 mile east to the original Tucki Mine cabin.

The next overview worth mentioning, is accessed by passing the Tucki Mine, again driving to the wilderness boundary, and hiking further down canyon. While I find the first overlook the better of the two, this one is still worth mentioning.

The Tucki Mine ruins consist of a barely standing head frame and ore chute, four-fifty ton leeching tanks, and concrete foundations. There is also the decrepit cabin,

The view of the main valley from Tucki Mountain.

and small out building. The cabin itself is from the late era of mining that transpired here in the 1970's. It contains full furnishings, but has begun to succumb to the elements, the roof having collapsed over half of the building. In the not so distant future, this cabin will likely become another pile of lumber – its weathered boards washing away down canyon in a flash flood.

The Tucki Mine was first discovered in 1909 by Henry W. Britt. It was later relocated by John Millett, Samuel E. Ball, and Charles G. Walker in 1927, but no records of production are available prior to 1937. The mine was operated on and off from 1937 – 1975(ish), often by a lessee, and with little to no profit. Leading me to believe that the miners were also there for the view.

Dilapidated cabin at the Tucki Mine.

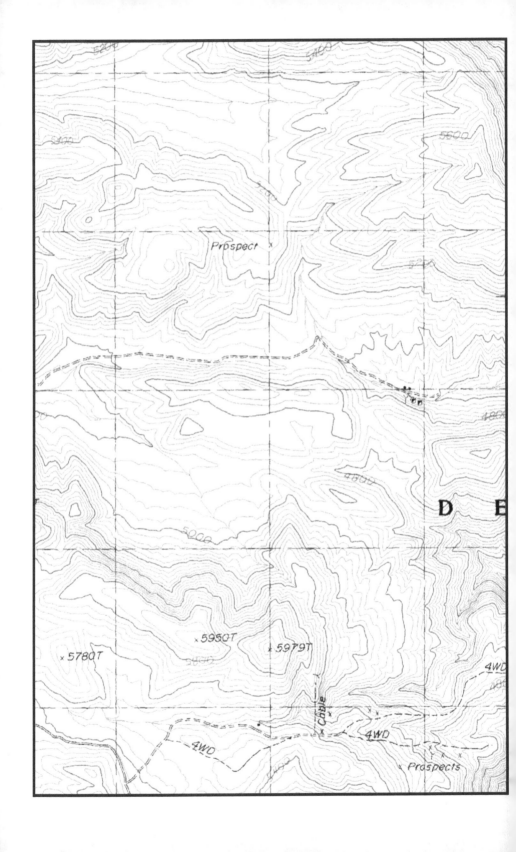

"What makes the desert beautiful is that somewhere it hides a well."

-Antoine De Saint-Exupery

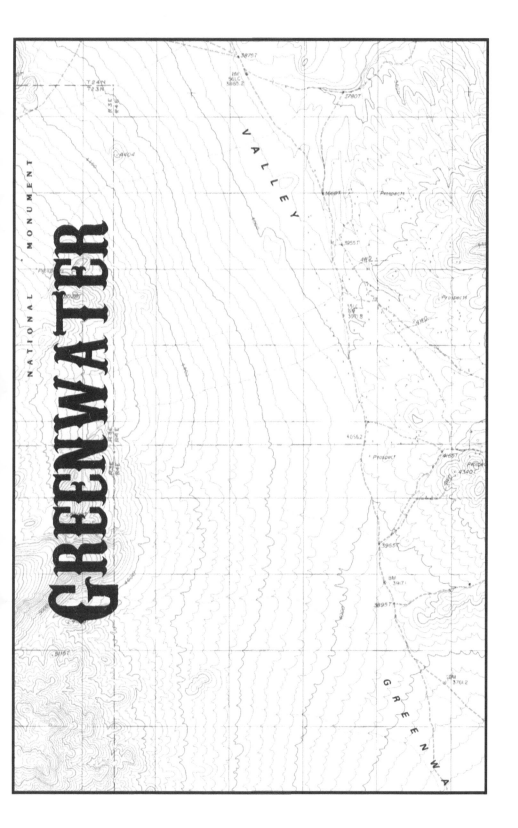

FUNERAL PETROGLYPHS

GPS Coordinates: 36° 6'50.66"N 116°35'38.93"W

Finding rock art in Death Valley can be downright frustrating. The amount of land that the park encompasses is a whopping 5,219 square miles, with 91% of that being wilderness! Both petroglyph and pictograph sites are rarely talked about, or written about – making it appear as if few of these sites exist in the park's land mass. In reality there are many, possibly hundreds, and very likely thousands of them. Most are small, containing a few small panels, while others contain hundreds of panels. Finding out where these precious messages in stone are located can take hours of research, and miles of hiking.

This particular site sits along the eastern base of Funeral Mountain, it is only reachable by means of a two-mile trek across Greenwater Valley. Keep in mind that this hike would not make an ideal summertime hike. Greenwater Valley is void of shade, placing you in the direct line of the sun for the duration of the hike.

I got a late start on my hike across Greenwater Valley, not arriving to where I had planned to begin my hike until roughly noon. It was the final days of December, which meant that my daylight was cut considerably short. The temperature was a frigid 36 degrees, I was bundled up in several layers of clothing, including my bulky Columbia jacket. My original intention was to visit this petroglyph site, then continue up to Funeral Peak. I realized right away that I wouldn't have time to visit Funeral Peak, but I at least wanted to get out to the petroglyphs.

Bighorn Sheep petroglyphs.

The bulk of the hike only took about an hour, but having this massive mountain in my sights as my target, made it feel much longer. Every time that I would look up to see my progress, Funeral Mountain never appeared to get any closer. Needless to say, but the desert is a trickster.

Finally with the mouth of the canyon in my line of vision, I came across the first petroglyph boulder. It sat along the embankment of the wash; created by storms that have pummeled the mountain range over the past thousands/millions of years. The years of weathering, with no protection have not been kind to the pecked designs. The lines appear to all run together, leaving a rather jumbled, discernible mess.

With just a few hundred feet to go before reaching the mouth of the canyon, my anticipation grew immensely. I could clearly see that the canyon was jam-packed with black basalt, which can be a telling sign that petroglyphs are near. Immediately upon entering the canyon, I found what I had come here seeking. Several beautiful panels of bighorn sheep, elongated human figures, a sun glyph, squiggles, along with several more abstract designs. Their condition was pristine – vandalism free.

I climbed up the boulders to allow myself a better angle to photograph the designs. Deciding to sit there for a bit, I watched out over Greenwater Valley. I pondered the location of this particular location. Why here, what was the significance?\

Sitting there, it came to me – I could envision it in my mind. This was a travel route. From the Death Valley side of the Funeral Mountains, the Timbisha Shoshone would travel up the Funeral Mountains, and from the mouth of this canyon, they would exit

Looking out across Greenwater Valley.

the range. From here, they would cross Greenwater Valley, then descend Greenwater Canyon into the Greenwater Range. That would add some explanation to the large petroglyph and pictograph sites in Greenwater Canyon.

Interesting enough, later that evening I would be reading Nicholas Clapps book, "Old Magic". Clapp speaks of the Shoshone shaman(s), and their travel route from Death Valley, across Funeral Peak, and down Greenwater Canyon. While I feel that Clapp's book is based more on opinion than fact, I was excited to find that somebody else essentially had the same theory that I had come up with.

Once my mind returned to the present day, I climbed back down and searched for additional panels. There were a few – a sun wheel design, a spiral, and a couple of additional sheep. In general the site was small in number of designs, but strong in the spiritual sense. I say strong in the spiritual sense, because it isn't all that often that I essentially see the past happening. That sort of experience is only reserved for places that remain unmolested.

I returned on the path that originally led me here, but now seeing it in a different light – it wasn't just two-miles of empty landscape, it was two-miles with a purpose. This was a trail which lead to and from Tupippuh Nummu (Shoshone for "Our Homeland"), and it was walked for many years before my people invaded this sacred country.

Elongated anthropomorphic figure, along with several other designs.

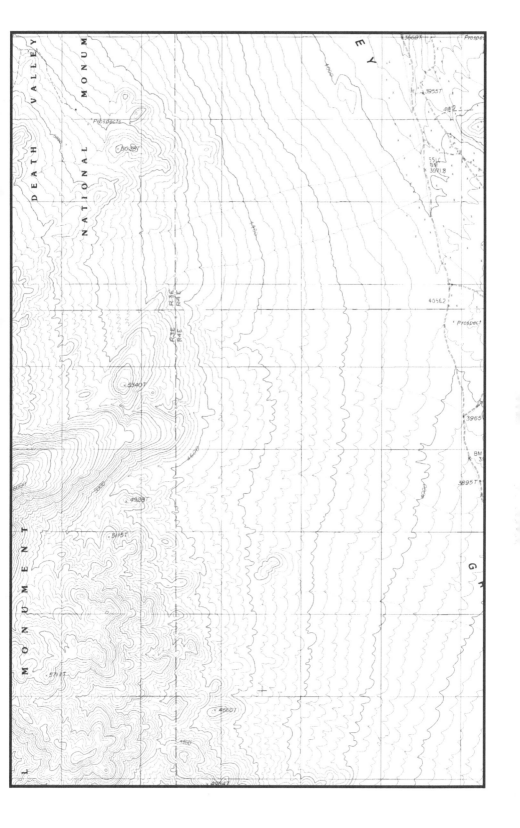

GREENWATER CANYON PETROGLYPHS

GPS Coordinates: 36°10'3.82"N 116°33'30.64"W

The petroglyphs in Greenwater Canyon is one of the more well-known "rock art" sites in Death Valley National Park. Despite that, they remain seldom visited due to their somewhat isolated location. This wasn't always the case, up until the California Desert Protection Act of 1994, a road once wound its way through Greenwater Canyon. The road was called "Petro Road", named after the petroglyphs that adorn the basalt walls in the canyon.

The Petro Road closure has been considered controversial. The road had been maintained by Inyo County as a "highway" up until its closure by the National Park Service. Inyo County sued the National Park Service, and the Department of the Interior for restricting access, and made plans to build a two-lane paved highway through the canyon. In June of 2007, a federal court upheld the closure, and the road remains closed to this day.

The road closure does not restrict hiking in to view the petroglyphs, with their location being a mere one mile from Furnace Creek Wash Road, it isn't a difficult task. From the barricades which close Petro Road, follow the sandy wash along the basalt rock hillside. The first petroglyphs begin to appear after about a half mile, with the highest concentration being near the one mile point.

There are roughly a couple of hundred designs pecked into the black basalt. A common theme among the panels is the atlatl, or rather a throwing stick. It is a piece of hunting weaponry, which predates the bow and arrow. The atlatl was known to have been replaced by the bow and arrow in this region between 200 BC and AD 500. This dates the petroglyphs to a period between then, or earlier.

The petroglyph designs are not limited to the atlatl, but also include a significant number of abstract designs in the form of circles, squiggles, lines, and interesting shapes. What the site lacks are anthropomorphic figures, and contains only a handful of zoomorphic figures.

It can be assumed that the Shoshone people, who have inhabited the region for thousands of years, once used Greenwater Canyon as connection between Death Valley, or "Tupippuh Nummu" (Shoshone for "Our Homeland"), and points further to the east.

If one continues down Greenwater Canyon, toward Death Valley Junction, there are additional petroglyph sites, and the Greenwater pictograph site.

Greenwater Canyon

A magnificat panel of large petroglyphs in Greenwater Canyon.

A very large panel consisting of mostly lines, and boxes.

An example of vandalism. Someone attempted to cut this bighorn sheep petroglyph out of the rock.

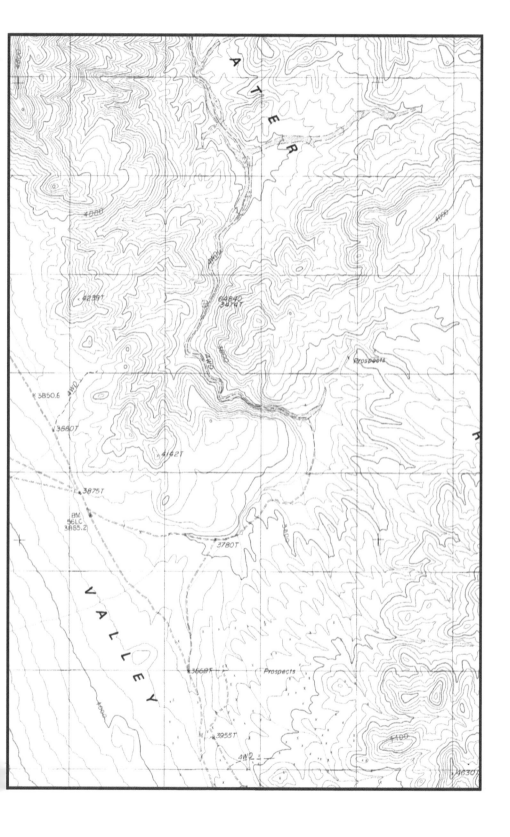

GREENWATER CANYON PICTOGRAPHS

GPS Coordinates: 36°12'22.74"N 116°34'7.02"W

It was a cold morning pulling out of Beatty, NV. So far my entire multiday trip had been plagued with chilly temperatures – it was only mid-October, I hadn't expected fall to have fully set in yet – but it had. I don't like the cold, but most consider this "desert camping season", I prefer to think of it as hibernation season. I'm one of those weird ones, I like the heat of the summer; give me 110 degrees any day over the 50s and 60s.

On this day, I was joined by my desert rat pal, Desert Mike from Joshuatreecamping.com. We left Beatty with Greenwater Valley as our intended destination. From there, we would make our way down Greenwater Canyon in search of several panels of polychrome pictographs.

The drive from Beatty to Greenwater, had us second guessing our days plans. From the time that we reached Amargosa Valley, we watched a stationary torrential downpour happening over the Resting Spring Range. We kept a close eye on the storm, to ensure that it wasn't heading in the direction of the Funeral Range, the mountains range that we would be hiking in. Even once entering Greenwater Valley, and making the several mile drive to the entrance of Greenwater Canyon, we were unsure – so we sat and waited. It is important to note that hiking in canyons during storms can be very dangerous. A flash flood can come out of nowhere, taking you by surprise, and sweeping you away.

We waited nearly an hour before deciding that the coast was clear. We started our hike the difficult way. Instead of traveling down the wash and into the canyon, we climbed a nearby hill and walked the ridge line of the Greenwater Range. The view of mountain range, and the Panamint Mountains in the distance was inspiring. We soon reached a point that left us with no other option than to drop down into Greenwater Canyon.

Once in the canyon our view became obstructed by high basalt cliffs, and treacherous rocky canyon walls. Interesting enough, at one time you could drive this route, but no longer. The road was closed several years back by the National Park Service, and the canyon is now designated wilderness.

On a ridge (36°12'7.94"N 116°33'35.77"W) we noticed several large, gnarly looking boulders. They reminded me of the deeply pitted volcanic boulders at the Counsel Rocks Archaeological site in the Mojave National Preserve. Our curiosity was peeked, causing us to inspect them up close. As we approached the boulders it became visible that they contained large hollow opening at their base, and stone circles had been placed around the openings. Their location being in such close proximity to a mining community that once had a population of over 2,000, we were skeptical. Closer examination revealed very rough, almost non visible petroglyphs carved into the pitted surface of the boulders. Bingo, we had found a habitation site.

Scouring the area we found several smaller basalt boulders adorned with ancient symbols (petroglyphs), as well a couple of metates. The presence of the metates provided additional proof that this was indeed a habitation or village site. A metate is a grounded flat stone surface, that was used to grind plants, nuts, and sometimes small animals – essentially a primitive kitchen.

After documenting our finds, we continued further down the canyon. We knew we were close to the pictographs, but were unsure of which side canyon we would find them in. The first canyon that we attempted proved to be incorrect, but a good work out – consisting of an assortment dry falls and large boulder scrambles.

We back tracked to a canyon that we had previously passed, if we had only inspected it better before passing it by, we would have found a faint trail leading up the side of the canyon. The trail was long and windy, so long that I began to think that we had been bamboozled, but we were now fully dedicated to the trail. Several twists and turns later we found ourselves overlooking Greenwater Canyon, along with a stunning view of Amargosa Valley, Death Valley Junction, and Eagle Mountain.

Looking to the ground revealed thousands of stone flakes from flint knapping, the ancient craft of creating dart points, and blades. We soon came upon two large rock shelter, adorned with the polychrome pictographs that we had set out to find. Images in white, red, black, and even yellow – anthropomorphic (images depicting humans), and zoomorphic (images depicting animals) depictions.

One of the pictograph shelters in Greenwater Canyon.

Like the pictographs that are located at several other sites in the Death Valley vicinity, the Greenwater site is considered to be of the Coso painted style. These designs are not as ancient as a lot of other pictographs, or even petroglyphs. This conclusion has been made due to the depictions in the designs. Several of the depictions are of men on horseback, and long horn cattle. This subject matter wouldn't have been introduced to the Native people until white men entered this region, in which the earliest would have been 1849.

While a specific date period is unknown, it is possible that the Native people inhabited this site during, or just before the Greenwater mining boom. It is also quiet possible, like that of the Panamint City Pictograph Shelter, the designs had been made after the desertion of the mining communities. The tribal people who were probably associated with this site, were the Panamint Shoshone, now known as the Timbisha Shoshone – they still call Death Valley their home today.

While these sites remain shrouded in mystery, they are a fascinating look at early life in a harsh climate.

We spent an hour or so with the spirits, before trudging our way back up Greenwater Canyon, arriving back at the Jeep just as the sun disappeared from the sky.

Bighorn sheep pictographs. Note their forward facing horns, this is an unusual design for the region.

Eagle Mountain as seen from Greenwater Canyon.

Mortars under the shelter. Lens cap for scale.

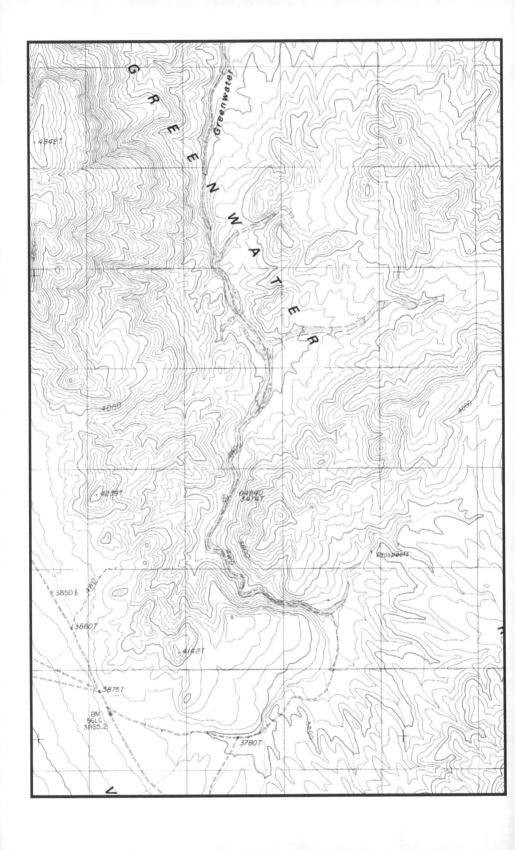

"The desert surrounds your every step and you walk forever a thirsty man."

-Christopher Pike

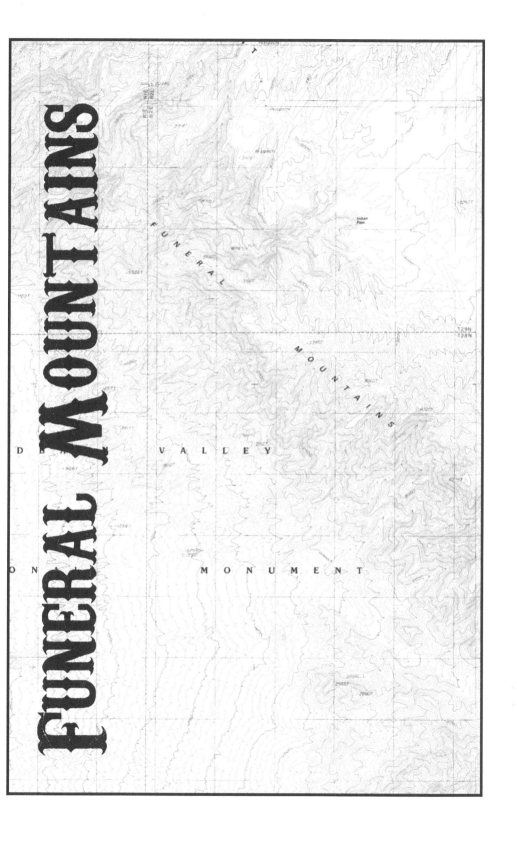

CHLORIDE CITY & CHLORIDE CLIFF

GPS Coordinates: 36°42'10.32"N 116°52'55.14"W

Chloride City was one of the first communities to have formed in Death Valley. The Chloride Cliff Mine was discovered in August of 1871, by A. J. Franklin, an engineer employed by the U.S. Government. Legend has it that Franklin was out surveying the Nevada/California border line, when he came upon a rattlesnake. He picked up a stone to throw at the snake, and found what he thought was a vein of silver. Franklin wasted no time, he staked seven claims, and in October formed the Chloride Cliff Mining Company.

In April of the following year, Franklin began working his claims. In July, he was employing seven miners. The shaft was down seventy feet, and he had nearly 100 tons of ore ready for shipment. The facilitating of these ore shipments proved to be problematic. No roads had been built through Death Valley that lead to civilization, and yet Franklin was dependent on San Bernardino, which was 180 miles away.

The process of creating a route through Death Valley to San Bernardino proved to be lengthy, and pack trains would arrive at the Chloride Mines about once every three months. The significant cost of shipping ore got to be too much, making it nearly impossible to attract investors. Finally after two years, Franklin was forced to shut down the Chloride Cliff Mining Company.

Franklin and his venture, despite failing to provide a financial gain for Franklin, had a profound effect on mining in Death Valley. The road that had been carved out in order to reach the Chloride Mines from San Bernardino began to be used and improved by the large borax mines in the years that followed.

Franklin never abandoned his mines completely, despite not working them regularly, he returned every year to do the required assessment work, until he died in 1904. Franklin's son, George E. Franklin, kept the tradition going after his father's death.

Soon after George took over the mines, the Bullfrog Hills boom happened, and the mining boom at Rhyolite and the Bullfrog Hills in southwest Nevada was in full swing. With Rhyolite becoming an overnight boom town, George seized the opportunity to reopen the Chloride Cliff Mines. This new opportunity provided George the ability to mine and ship ore at a profit, unlike his father.

Before long prospectors made their way from the busy Bullfrog Hills to the Chloride Cliff area in search of new prospects. In September of 1905, the Bullfrog Mining District was created, and the Chloride Cliff area was included in this newly formed district.

Chloride Cliff was soon inundated with new mining ventures. Mucho Oro Mining Company began operations in April of 1905, the Bullfrog Cliff Mining Company was formed in October, and the Death Valley Mining and Milling Company in November. Between these three companies and George Franklin's holdings, they owned the best ground in the Chloride Cliff area. Between the big four, the ore value averaged around $50 per ton.

With so many miners and so much action happening within the vicinity, it was only natural for a town to be born; 1905 saw the birth of Chloride City. The town was situated in a saddle, 4,800 feet above Death Valley. During winter months this area of the Funeral Mountains had its share of cold blistering wind, and even snow. There was no water available locally for the miners and mines, it was packed in from three miles away at Keane Springs. Lumber for the building of structures was also packed in from up to 10 miles away.

Despite having little in the way of businesses or conveniences, it was thought that Chloride City may become the next boom town. The few businesses that did exist where a blacksmith shop, an assay office, a cookhouse, and a bunkhouse.

In April of 1906, the San Francisco earthquake and fire occurred, this caused a scare in the mining industry, as it was unsure what kind of financial crisis an event of this magnitude would cause. Little work was done during April and May, and by June the only company operating at Chloride Cliff was the Death Valley Mining and Milling Company.

An "improved" cousin-jack dug-out.

Chloride City circa 1914.

Joshua Irving Crowell in his dugout dwelling at his Chloride Cliff mine. October of 1915.

For George Franklin, this was the end of the road. He sold his mine, and claims that had been in his family since 1871, to a Pittsburgh based mining outfit for a reported sum of $150,000.00. Death Valley Mining and Milling, as well as the other companies that had been working the area all folded in July, and all the mines went idle.

Chloride City and it's mines became a ghost town by mid-1906 and remained that way until the end of 1909. During this long hiatus all the Chloride Cliff mines had been consolidated and purchased by Pennsylvania based company, Pennsylvania Mining and Leasing Company. The Pennsylvania company had much success with the Chloride mines, they expanded the operation regularly, but by April of 1911, they had done so much expansion that they didn't have a clue what their next move was. So they sold it...

J. Irving Crowell, of London was the purchaser. Crowell did little work after the purchase, mostly just the required annual assessment work. The mines of the Chloride Cliff, lied almost idle until 1928 when Crowell sold to Louis McCrea, of Beatty, NV.

McCrea, worked the mines for a short period before leasing the mines to the newly formed, Chloride Cliff Mining & Milling Company. The new company had big plans, but as usual, didn't follow through.

The grave of James McKay.

Small amounts of mining took place for the next thirteen years, but all operations appear to have come to a stop in 1941, and Chloride City and it's mines would slip into history.

Today very little remains of Chloride City, a few old cabins hang on by a needle thread, most have been reduced to nothing more than a pile of old boards. The mines have been sealed by the National Park Service for our safety (sarcasm). The grave site of James McKay, a man that nobody knows anything about sits lonely at the old town site.

The most impressive thing at Chloride City today are the spectacular views of Death Valley, that rival those of Dante's Peak and Aguereberry Point, and the somewhat scary, yet thrilling road that leads you there.

The view of Death Valley from Chloride Cliff.

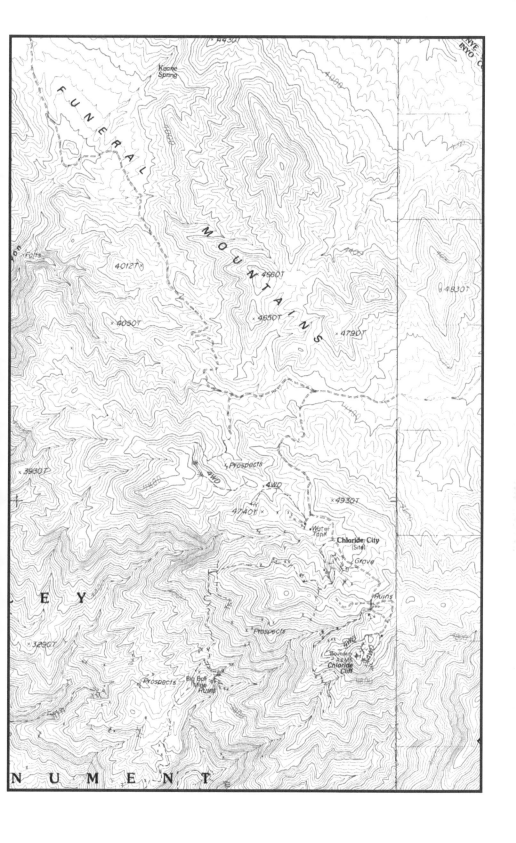

ECHO CANYON PETROGLYPHS

GPS Coordinates: 36°29'58.08"N 116°40'48.19"W

Echo Canyon in the Funeral Mountains has it all – from an incredible arch, towering canyon walls, to mines, ghost towns, and yes even "rock art". In the near future I am planning a "featured report" on Echo Canyon; from the mouth of the canyon to the ghostly ruins of an unnamed mining camp in upper-Echo Canyon. For now however, we are going to take a brief look at the petroglyphs of Echo Canyon.

It is unfortunate how tight-lipped Death Valley National Park is with their archeological research. Very few research papers on the region are publicly available, which make it difficult to present the hard facts on many of these sites. In this author's opinion this provides a disservice to the tribe, and to the general public. Overly generic or no public information leads to false assumptions, and hurts the tribal history of the region. It is also in the author's opinion that the NPS's failure to educate the public on "rock art" is the number one reason these sites get defaced.

Due to that lack of information available, I am going to keep my text brief.

The Echo Canyon petroglyphs can be accessed with a short half-mile hike past one of the canyon's wilderness road closures. I can only assume, that this wilderness

Petroglyphs in Echo Canyon.

boundary was placed in an effort to keep people from visiting this very interesting petroglyph site. But don't fret, wilderness only stops entry by vehicle, and foot traffic is welcome.

The hike is simple, following the closed dirt road through the canyon wash. Once the road peters out, just continue to follow the wash. There are no side canyons, so ones ability to get lost is minimal. Pay particular attention to the geology, the stone is mostly jagged and upheaved out of the ground, and contains very interesting, and beautiful stripped patterns.

You've finally reached the petroglyphs when you round a bend, containing a number of large polished boulders in the wash. Both the north and south walls of the canyon contain petroglyphs, but the highest concentration can be found on the southern wall, above ground level on the jagged slabs of stone. The best way to view the panels is to climb up the canyon face, being careful not to step on or handle any of the rock carvings.

The panels contain a couple of hundred small-medium designs, ranging from stick-figure anthropomorphs, rakes, circles, pitchforks, and water or rain squiggles. Noticeably scarce at the site are zoomorphic figures, with the exception of a few bighorn sheep heads, and a hybrid of a bighorn-human male figure.

Like most of the "rock art" in Death Valley, it was likely produced by members of the Timbisha Shoshone, ancestors of the Uto-Aztecans. It is widely believed that they came to the Death Valley region sometime in the past 1,000-2,000 years, and they continue to live in Death Valley to this day.

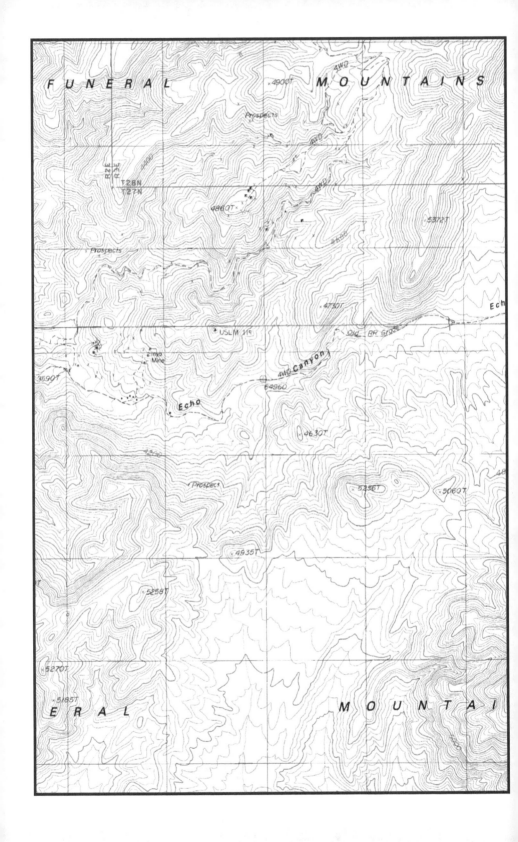

EYE OF THE NEEDLE

GPS Coordinates: 36°27'59.91"N 116°45'33.25"W

The Eye of the Needle in Death Valley's, Echo Canyon is a natural arch (or window) created by wind and water erosion over an extended period, causing chunks of the rock to fall from the tall canyon wall. The best vantage to view the arch is looking down canyon, back toward the valley proper, and the Panamint Mountains.

The arch can be found roughly 5.1 miles up the Echo Canyon Trail from Highway 190. Most of the time the road is well maintained with a few pockets of deeper sand, most high clearance vehicles won't have any issues making the trip to The Eye of Needle, or further up Echo Canyon to the Inyo Mine.

The Eye of the Needle in Echo Canyon.

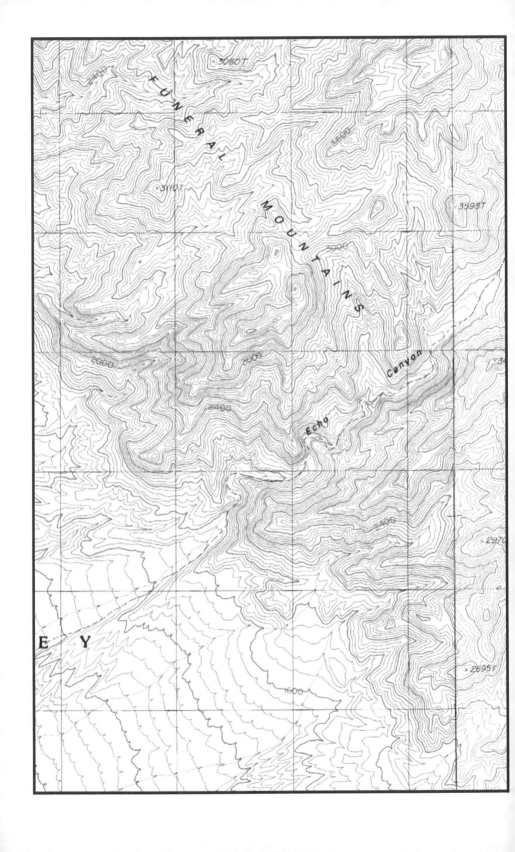

INYO MINE

GPS Coordinates: 36°29'36.55"N 116°42'13.85"W

The Echo Mining District was a far cry from being successful, and was mostly comprised of several small mines that never made it much further than the development stages. The Inyo Mine was by far the most successful mine in the district, but even saying that is like trying to call a turd a rose.

Discovered in 1905 by Maroni Hicks and Chet Leavitt, the pair's properties became the talk of the region – helping to create the short lived Echo Mining District boom. In August the duo received an offer to lease their claim from Tasker L. Oddie (who later went on to be a Senator from the State of Nevada) for $150,000, and Bethlehem Steel mogul, Charles Schwab for $100,000.

Oddie went to work right away on his portion of the claim. He and his men managed to develop a 50-foot shaft, before walking away from the property just two months later, in November of 1905. As for Schwab, he never made good on his payment, and his portion of the claim remained undeveloped.

Hicks and Leavitt, then leased the mine, to two Colorado capitalists. They too backed out quickly, without ever making a single payment.

In December, L. Holbrook and associates, a group of Utah mining promoters, pur-

The Inyo Mine after having been abandoned. Date unknown.

chased the entire mine for an undisclosed amount of money, and incorporated the Inyo Gold Mining Company. Hicks took a cash settlement, while Leavitt retained his half, and opted to become the Vice President of the company.

The Inyo Gold Mining Company spent the next six years at the helm of the Inyo Mine, with little success. The financial panic of 1907 didn't do the company any favors, having had just exhausted their working capital, and having gone public for the first time, in hopes of securing new funding.

The company had several men in employee over the years, and had even constructed a bunkhouse, and blacksmith shop.

In 1912, when the company abandoned the mine, it was estimated that three hundred and fifty feet worth of shaft work had been done, in addition to 700 feet of tunneling and 75 feet of crosscutting. No ore had ever been shipped.

From 1912 through around 1930, the Inyo Mine remained out of commission. It wasn't until 1937, under the ownership of a Mrs. Gilbert, with a lease to Inyo Consolidated Mining Company that the Inyo Mine was back in full operation.

A report from The California Journal of Mines & Geology stated the following in regard to the operation,"The Inyo Consolidated Mine was working on the seventeen patented and five unpatented claims of the property. The principle development was an inclined shaft, 220 feet deep. Ore from the mine, was averaging about $25 per ton, and was

What remains of the 25-ton ball mill.

being processed through the twenty-five ton capacity ball mill. The mill equipment consisted of a fifty ton ore bin, a six by ten jaw crusher, a thirty ton receiving bin, a reciprocating feeder, a three by six ball mill, amalgamation plates, two Simpson tables, and a drag classifier for dewatering. Water was still being hauled from Death Valley, and eight men were employed at the mine and mill."

A short time after The California Journal of Mines & Geology reported on the Inyo Mine, it was again abandoned due to lack of funding. In February of 1939, the Inyo Mine would again be leased, this time to an unnamed individual. This unnamed individual may have been the first to actually make money at the Inyo Mine, having found a rich vein of ore, shipped thirty-six tons of ore worth $280 per ton to the smelter, for a gross profit of $10,080. Once the vein ran out, so did his luck.

In 1940 the mine was leased one final time to Thomsen and Wright. They built a smelter on site, which they would only fire once.

While the significance of the Inyo Mine as a working mine is questionable, there is still much to see of the historic structures that had been built to support mining activities. These structures which remain on site are by far some of the easiest to access for a visitor to Death Valley National Park, located in Echo Canyon, several miles up an improved dirt road.

Amongst the still standing structures is the skeleton of the ball mill, which was constructed during the early 1900s. A large portion of the mill was scrapped over the

Dilapidated wooden structure, likely a workshop.

years, but the wood frame, diesel engine (which powered the mill), mixing vat, and various other elements remain in tact – providing for a opportunity to get a rough idea of what the mill once looked like.

Several building structures, tent platforms, and dug-outs also remain – allowing for a glimpse of the camp at its various stages throughout the 40 plus years of operation. The buildings are all in very rough condition, due to years of abandonment and neglect – but their state of decay adds an element of intrigue, which would likely be lost if a full-scale restoration would be performed.

The Inyo Mine is a worthy place to spend an hour or two, for those that are interested in the Death Valley mining era, and are unable to traverse the backcountry due to their vehicles lack of ability.

The bunk-house.

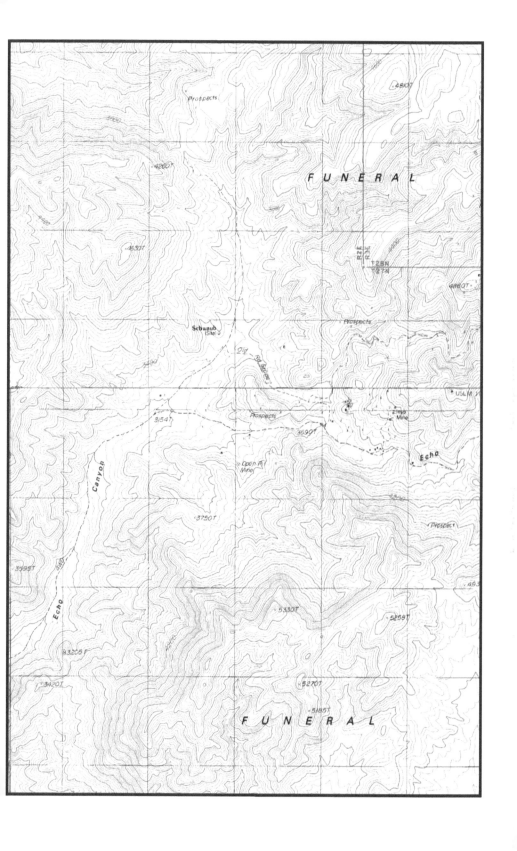

SCHWAB

GPS Coordinates: 36°30'13.70"N 116°43'21.30"W

Charles M. Schwab, is a name that was synonymous with the Pennsylvania steel empire of Bethlehem Steel. A side from the steel business, Schwab was an investor in many Death Valley area mines. One of his first endeavors in the Death Valley area was the Skibo Mine, and the incorporation of the Skibo Mining Company. Shortly thereafter, Schwab invested in the Greenwater District, and in the Montgomery Shoshone Mine in Rhyolite, NV – but those are other stories, not associated with the townsite of Schwab.

The town of Schwab was constructed in support of the Skibo Mine, and named in honor of the investor himself. In January of 1907, the town literally arrived via five boxcars, which consisted of several canvas style tent buildings. At that time, this was looked at as being modern for the era. It took about two months for the population to swell to around two-hundred residents, and along with the residents came a post-office, a miner's union hall, telephone service, and a daily stage to Rhyolite.

Somewhere along the line, three women by the names of Gertrude Fesler, F.W. Dunn, and Helen H. Black, took ownership of the small community. This was considered an oddity, and newspaper headlines across the region rang out with headlines like, "A Mining Camp Built by Ladies," said the Death Valley Chuck-Walla, and "One of the most unique wonders of the new West," said the Bullfrog Miner.

Schwab has been reduced to scattered ruins. No structures remain standing.

Along with the female ownership, came an odd clamp-down on gambling, drinking, and whoring. The Death Valley Chuck-Walla reported, "The gamblers were told to get out. Saloon men were frowned at and sporting women were positively refused entrance. Men said that a mining camp could not exist under such restrictions, but Schwab did. The women hastened to secure the post office, the first in the district, and everybody in the three towns [Schwab, Lee, California and Lee, Nevada] had to come to Schwab for mail."

Schwab eventually faltered, and only several months after its inception. The town of Lee provided much competition to Schwab, being located closer to the hub of Rhyolite, as well as looser morals, this combined with the Financial Panic of 1907, sealed Schwab's fate.

Having consisted of only tent structures, and no wood framed buildings, the location of the townsite was lost to history for a significant period of time. Records indicate that the actual location of Schwab wasn't reidentified until the 1970s, during historic research performed by Death Valley National Park. For the longest time, Schwab was thought to have existed below the Inyo Mine, and the remains of the town never found, having been swallowed up by the large mine site.

Thanks to the historic research of Death Valley historians, we now know that the townsite was situated, "in the north or upper branch of Echo Canyon, astride the main Echo-Lee wagon road, across a small ridge from the present Inyo ruins, and about 1-1/2 miles from those ruins."

Unidentified grave at Schwab.

Advertisement for the Schwab townsite in the March 1st, 1907 edition of the Bullfrog Miner.

Access to the old townsite is now restricted to foot traffic, so I set off on foot one fine December afternoon with the intentions of locating the site of Schwab. An old wagon road led through the upper branch of Echo Canyon, I followed this path as much as possible – at times it was difficult to follow, having been washed out in many places. Less than a mile from where I parked, I found the scant remains of Schwab, "A Mining Camp Built by Ladies."

Very little identifiable features are present, the ruins consisting largely of wood tent platforms, stone walls, and tin cans. A single grave lies across the way from one of the thrashed tent platforms, it is marked by a wooden cross, with the words "Death Valley Victim – 1907," carved into it. The authenticity of this grave is often debated, there being no recorded deaths during Schwab's short existence.

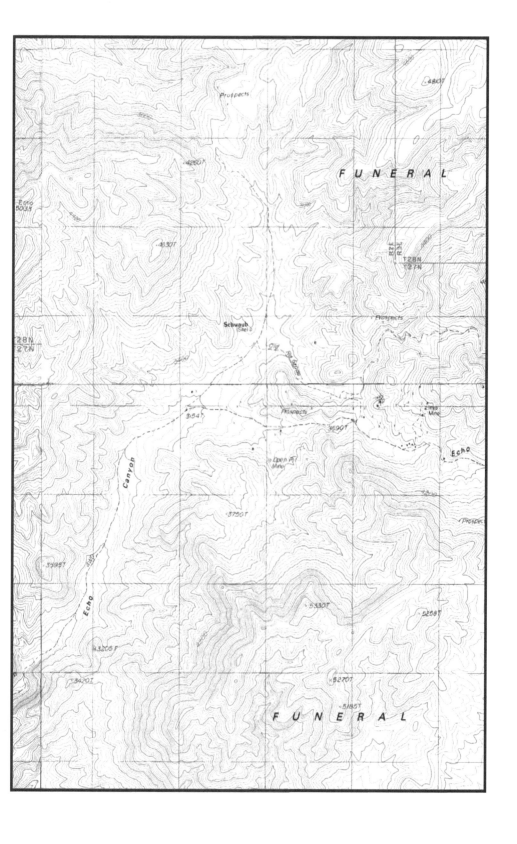

"The desert wears...a veil of mystery. Motionless and silent it evokes in us an elusive hint of something unknown, unknowable, about to be revealed. Since the desert does not act it seems to be waiting -- but waiting for what?"

-Edward Abbey

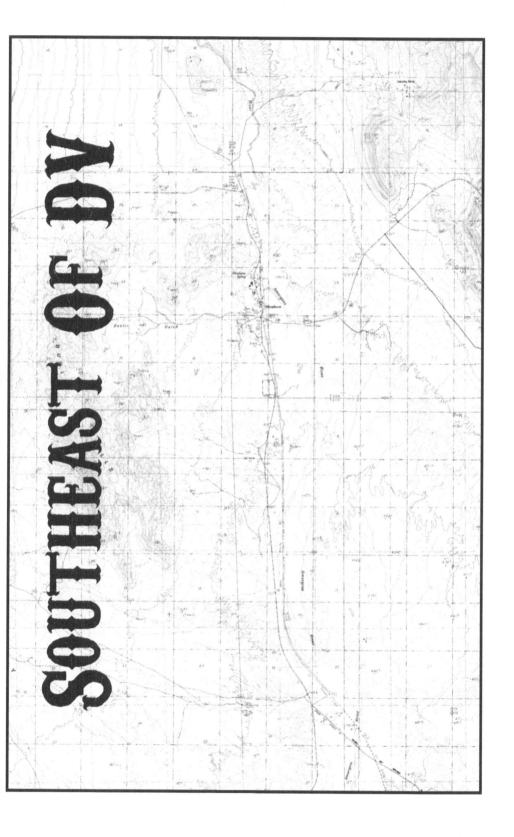

DEATH VALLEY JUNCTION

GPS Coordinates: 36°18'7.49"N 116°24'51.77"W

Death Valley Junction was originally named Amargosa ("bitter water" in Paiute language), the name was changed in 1907 because the Tonopah & Tidewater Railroad connected with the Las Vegas – Tonopah Railroad here to service the Ryan and Lilac C. Borax Mines near Ryan from 1914 – 1928. From 1923-1925 the Pacific Coast Borax Company constructed many buildings around the town including the Spanish Colonial Revival whistle stop which included a hotel, theater, and office building.

In 1927, Pacific Coast Borax relocated to Boron, CA. Boron would serve (and still does) as the new mining location for PCB (now known as Rio Tinto Borax). This didn't seem to matter much at the time, Death Valley Junction continued to thrive as a tourist spot. Once the mines at New Ryan closed up, so did the railroad with the exception of the baby gauge railroad that ran from New Ryan into the Widow Maker and Charley McCarthy Mines. This baby gauge remained open into the 1950's, not for mining, but for tourist rides.

In 1967 a breath of fresh air arrived in Death Valley Junction, her name Marta Becket. Marta, a New York ballet dancer, mime and artist had been traveling with her husband in Death Valley. One morning they awoke to find that they had a flat tire. A park ranger sent them to a repair shop in Death Valley Junction. Marta's husband attended to the

The Amargosa Opera House, as it is seen today.

tire, while Marta walked around the sleepy town. While exploring she came upon the abandoned theater (Corkhill Hall), which was part of the Spanish Colonial Revival whistle stop. She instantly feel in love with it. The next day they tracked down the owner and agreed to rent the building for $45.00 per month.

Today that building is known as the Amargosa Opera House, Marta performed at the Opera House for the better part of 45 years, only officially retiring in 2014. The Opera House is much quieter these days, however an occlusional show makes its way to Death Valley Junction in the cooler months.

As well as the Opera House, Marta operates a hotel and café. Some people believe that the hotel and opera house are haunted by the miners that stayed here during the borax days. Multiple television specials have been filmed over the last few years on this subject, some are very convincing.

Death Valley Junction is now a very quiet place. At one time it had a population of three-hundred, but now is home to only four.

A number of abandoned structures remain, and the town cemetery alway makes for any interesting visit. The Tonopah & Tidewater Railroad Museum is also located in Death Valley Junction, having opened their doors 2013.

Death Valley Junction in 1935.

Pacific Coast Borax in 1926. This building would become the Amargosa Hotel.

A Modern look at the same building as above. Now the Amargosa Hotel.

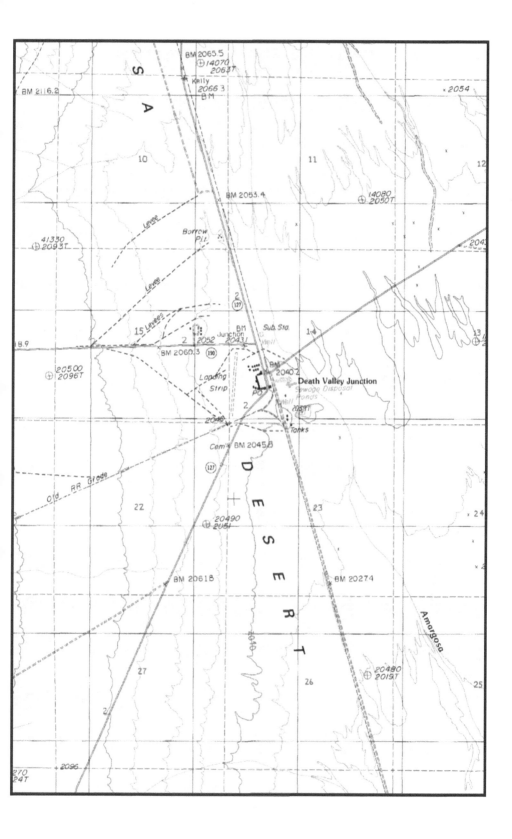

DUBLIN GULCH CAVES

GPS Coordinates: 35°58'24.08"N 116°16'28.36"W

The Dublin Gulch caves are in the town of Shoshone, CA. The caves are dug out of volcanic ash from a Lava Creek eruption in Yellow Stone National Park, over six-hundred thousand years ago. It is unknown when the caves where dug out and first inhabited, it was likely to have been in the late 1870's during the silver boom at the Noonday Mines. The caves have been home to many people over the years, most of them local miners. The caves remained occupied at some extent well into the 1970's.

Over the years the people living here upgraded their dwellings to include gas stoves, ice boxes, wood floors, shelving, and more. When residents of the caves died, or moved on the other residents would quickly move to the empty cave if it was more spacious or had more amenities.

There is no official record of the residents that have lived here, but a partial list includes:

Jack Norman
"Squaw Tom"
"Dobie Charlie" Nels (Prospector / Miner)

The dugout homes in Dublin Gulch.

Joe Volmer (Miner)
Jack Crowly (Miner)
Jack Norman "Deafie Jack"
Henry Ashford (Miner)
Harold or Louis Ashford (Brother of Henry...unclear which brother lived here with Henry) (Miner)
"Papa Jim"
James F. Dallas (Miner)
Johnny Sheridan (Miner)
Joseph W. Allison
James Frederick Belfield
"Whitey" Staley
"Shorty" O'Bannon
Oscar Haskins

It is also rumored that Shorty Harris may have lived in the caves off and on during the years.

Today you can walk around the cave community, however all of the dwellings are now under lock and key. Most do have windows allowing you the opportunity to look inside, but nothing more. Adjacent to the cave dwellings is the Shoshone Cemetery where you will find some past residents of the cave dwellings resting alongside many of the founding members of the Shoshone community.

The dugouts have doors, and others have stone wall features as seen here.

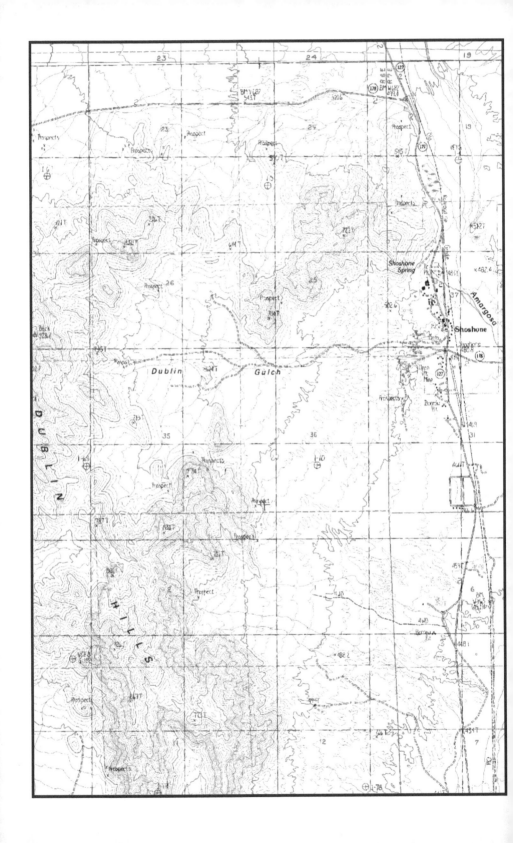

NOONDAY MINES & CAMP

GPS Coordinates:
Noonday Camp: 35°48'37.77"N 116° 6'15.71"W
War Eagle Mine: 35°49'14.75"N 116° 5'28.85"W
Oro Fino Mine: 35°49'31.72"N 116° 5'33.54"W
Noonday Mine: 35°49'47.04"N 116° 5'47.12"W
Columbia Mine: 35°49'35.14"N 116° 6'5.31"W

The Noonday mines are located in the Alexander Hills, roughly seven miles southeast of modern-day Tecopa. "Noonday mines" refer to several silver-lead mines, which include the Noonday, War Eagle, Gunsight, and Columbia.

The mines were discovered in 1875 by the Brown brothers, but were quickly bought out by Jonas Osborne in 1877. Osbourne and company operated the mines until 1881.

During the earliest days of mining, Noonday Camp had yet to be established. The miners lived at the original Tecopa location, just a short distance away from where Noonday Camp would later be built. In 1907 the Tonopah & Tidewater Railroad was constructed through Amargosa Canyon. The Tecopa town site was moved as a result to its current modern-day location, requiring longer commutes for the men working at the Noonday properties.

From 1907-1928 the Noonday mines operated under Lincoln D. Godshall. Under his administration the mines became profitable. That wasn't however be the last time that the Noonday group would change hands. In the 1940's, The Finley Company took over the mining operations, and built Noonday Camp to provide housing for the miners in their employ.

Again the mines changed hands in the late 1940's. The Anaconda Mining Company purchased and operated the mines until 1957. Western Talc would then take over in 1957 and be the last mining operation at the Noonday mines, closing their doors in 1972.

Little remains at Noonday Camp for being a relatively newer ghost town. The only remaining structure that still stands at the town site is the cinder block vault that was used to hold the company script, which was used to pay the miners. Roughly twenty foundations can be stumbled upon when searching the brush, along with a small graveyard.

Many of the mines in the Noonday group are popular for exploration amongst mining enthusiasts and underground explorer groups.

The only still standing structure at Noonday Camp is this vault.

Collapsed trestle at the Oro Fino.

Inside the War Eagle Mine.

Ore chute at the Noonday Mine.

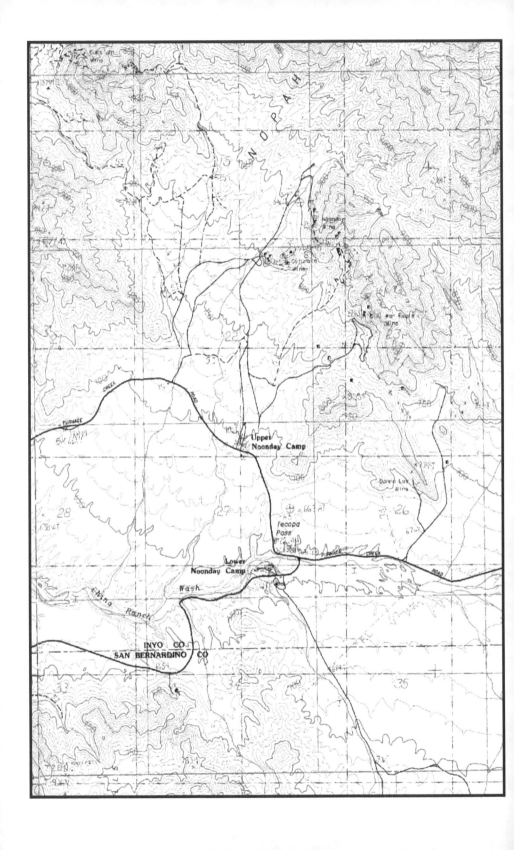

RESTING SPRING PASS WELDED TUFF

GPS Coordinates: 35°59'49.74"N 116°13'9.91"W

Approximately 3.7 miles outside of Shoshone, CA, along Highway 178 a cut was placed in a hillside during the construction of the highway. Road workers had to have been surprised to find that they had uncovered a black strip of rock during the blasting process. But is it rock? Or possibly coal? Actually it is neither, the strip of black is welded tuff (ie: volcanic glass).

Welded Tuff is formed when a large amount of hot, gas-rich magma is blown from a volcano. The foamy material consists of glassy particles called pumice. Pumice ranges in size from dust to large blocks, and it can reach temperatures over 1,300 degrees fahrenheit. The foamy material flows across the landscape beneath a grey cloud of ash. The top and bottom layers of ash cool rather quickly, but the center remained hot; this allowed it to weld together, creating the amazing black vein of glass that we see today.

Geologist have dated the tuff to 9.5 million years old, using radiometric dating.

A small dirt pull-off is located directly across from the welded tuff, allowing for easy access to the site.

The black streak is the welded tuff, or volcanic glass.

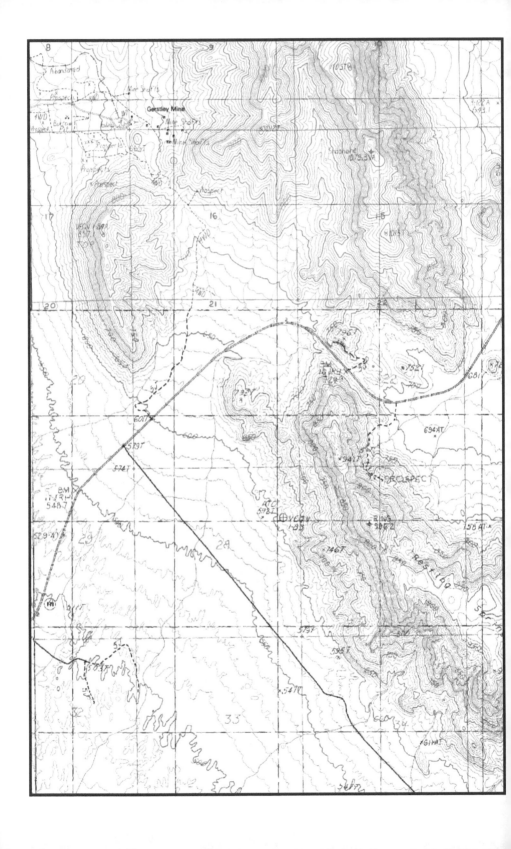

TECOPA (OLD) AKA. BROWNSVILLE

GPS Coordinates: 35°48'0.79"N 116° 6'5.09"W

William D. and Robert D. Brown discovered good ore south of Resting Springs, along the Old Spanish Trail in 1875. They partnered with wealthy business man George Hearst, and created the Balance Consolidated Gold and Silver Mining Company.

The Brown brothers wasted no time in laying out a townsite, calling it Brownsville. Brownsville was located along Willow Creek, about six miles southeast of Resting Springs.

Jonas Osborne, a mining superintendent out of Hamilton, NV learned of the strike. He purchased the claims and townsite from Balance Consolidated, renaming the town Tecopa, after Chief Tecopa, a Paiute Indian that was known as a peacemaker for his part in stopping Paiute attacks on travelers along the Old Spanish Trail.

The town grew to a substantial size. Lots sold for up to $75, and a post office and saloon served the community. It was at this same time that Tecopa was added to Inyo County, for tax purposes.

The original site of the town of Tecopa.

Old Tecopa was for the most part abandoned in 1879, a new townsite had been established several miles to the west. The post office continued to operate in old Tecopa until 1881.

Today the site of old Tecopa is owned by the Amargosa Conservancy, with a goal of preserving it in its current state. The only structure that remains at the site is an old dilapidated mill.

Mill at old Tecopa.

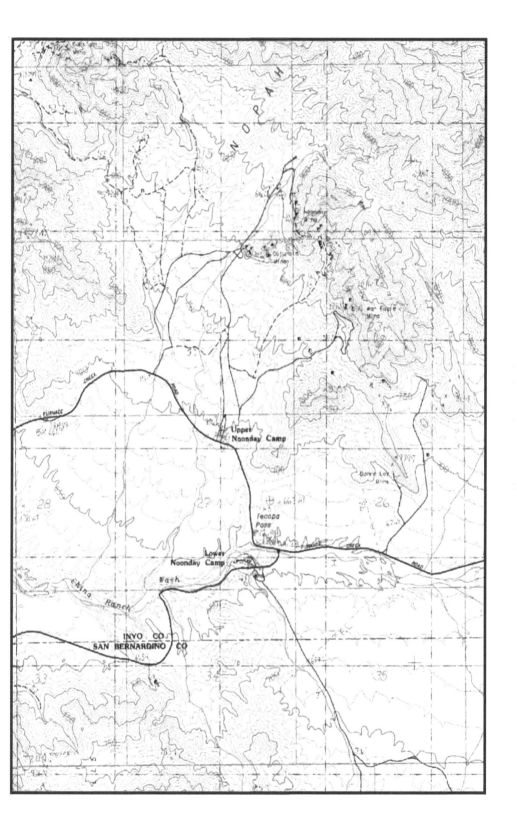

HISTORIC PHOTO ARCHIVE

Death Valley in 1932.

A remnant of an old emigrants outfit left by the emigrants who perished while attempting to cross Death Valley in 1850.

Wikiups in Death Valley April 1931. Wikiups were built by local Indian tribes for shelter.

In 1876 Government Surveyors found this old wagon in the valley north of "Emigrant Wash". Since then this place has been marked on the maps as "Last Wagon".

Body of an unidentified person found in Death Valley in 1908.

Crossing the Devil's Golf Course. Photo 1926

Airport in Death Valley. Photo 1932

Indian Village at Furnace Creek. Photo 1940

Cow Creek in the 1920's was a camp for the CCC. Today it houses many of the park rangers.

Eichbaum Toll Road from Stove Pipe Wells in 1926. This road is now Highway 190.

Wa-Pai-Shone Trading Post In the Death Valley Indian Village; 1940. Today the reservation no longer operates a trading post.

An early image of Greenland Ranch.

Pacific Coast Borax Office in Twenty Mule Team Canyon - 1941. This building now houses the Borax Museum at Furnace Creek.

For trip reports, historic information, photographs, and more, visit the author online at:

www.deathvalleyjim.com

www.facebook.com/deathvalleyjim

Other books by Death Valley Jim

Secret Places in the Mojave Desert
Volume I

Secret Places in the Mojave Desert
Volume II

Secret Places in the Mojave Desert
Volume III

Secret Places in the Mojave Desert
Volume IV

Exploring Death Valley
Secret Places in the Mojave Desert
Volume V

Hidden Joshua Tree:
The Real Guide to Joshua Tree
National Park

Order at:
www.deathvalleyjim.com

Made in United States
Troutdale, OR
11/09/2024

24593906R00096